U.S. SMALL BUSINESS ADMINISTRATION
WASHINGTON, D.C. 20416

Dear 8(a) Program Participant:

We are pleased to provide a copy of *Gems of Wisdom for Increasing 8(a) BD Competitiveness*. Part of a series of *Gems of Wisdom* books– this publication provides valuable information for increasing the competitiveness of 8(a) firms in the federal contracting market and beyond.

The 8(a) Business Development Program offers a number of benefits for participating 8(a) firms. However, in order to take full advantage of these opportunities, 8(a) Participants must understand the rules and regulations governing the manner in which the federal government contracts for commodities and services. Equally important, is an understanding of resources available to assist you in your business growth and knowing how to utilize these resources to increase your competitiveness. The more knowledge you possess of the federal procurement system, the greater your chances of winning and successfully performing government contracts will be.

This book is intended to equip you with the necessary tools to achieve success while in the 8(a) Program and remain viable and competitive after you graduate.

Success upon graduation depends on how well you utilize the 8(a) Program while you are in it, and on the quality of your work and performance. Establishing a solid foundation while in the Developmental Stage of 8(a) Program Participation is crucial. The assistance provided by SBA, along with SBA's resource partners, and that of other agencies, will catapult you to a level of success beyond your expectations.

It is our hope that your success will pave the way for other 8(a) Participants and create an opportunity for you to participate as a mentor and impart value (through your experiences and "lessons learned") to developing 8(a) firms.

Sincerely,

Joseph P. Loddo
Associate Administrator
Office of Business Development

Enclosure

Gems of Wisdom
for
Increasing 8(a)BD Competitiveness

Sharon T. Freeman, Ph.D.

and

M. Charito Kruvant

AASBEA PUBLISHERS
2300 M STREET, NW
SUITE 800
Washington, DC 20037
Phone: (202) 332-5137
Fax: (202) 293-3083
Email: INFO@AASBEA.COM
Web: WWW.AASBEA.COM

Freeman, Sharon T. and Kruvant, M. Charito

Gems of Wisdom for Increasing 8(a)BD Competitiveness

Sharon T. Freeman, Ph.D. and M. Charito Kruvant
ISBN 978-0-9816885-0-3

1. Small Business
2. Small business development & small disadvantaged business
3. Minority small disadvantaged business development
4. Entrepreneurship
5. Government procurement & small business

I. Freeman, Sharon T. and Kruvant, M. Charito   II. Title.

Publisher:

AASBEA Publishers
All American Small Business Exporters Association, Inc.
2300 M Street, NW, Suite 800
Washington, DC 20037
Email: INFO@AASBEA.COM
Web: WWW. AASBEA.COM
Phone: (202) 332-5137
Fax: (202) 293-3083

Cover design and Graphic layout by Creative Services, Chester, Maryland

Gems of Wisdom for Increasing 8(a)BD Competitiveness

TABLE OF CONTENTS

Foreword

First and foremost, I regard the opportunity to provide the foreword to this important book a true honor.

Gems of Wisdom for Succeeding in the 8(a) BD Program and Beyond, the forerunner to this book, imparted brilliant *"gems of wisdom"* of some of the most successful 8(a) entrepreneurs, many of whom I have had the pleasure of working with over the years.

The numerous *"gems of wisdom"* contained in the previous publication covered the waterfront in highlighting what aspiring federal contractors should know and do to successfully navigate the federal procurement maze. A lot of the information was just plain old common sense, combined with a thorough understanding of the game. It's a must read for new kids on the block, and a reminder for others!

This sequel, *Gems of Wisdom for Increasing the Competitiveness of 8(a)BD Firms*, is also a must read, as it imparts *"gems of wisdom"* from the other side of the fence.

This book raises the voices of those who work with 8(a)BD contractors, which is important in completing the circle of knowledge about *"How to Do Business with the Federal Government."*

Collectively, in providing the perspectives of contractors who have navigated the federal maze—through the first *"gems of wisdom,"* and presenting the perspectives of those who are involved directly and indirectly in facilitating federal procurements, a road map for success is presented in this book.

No doubt, federal contracting can be lucrative but it requires an understanding of the complex and exacting procedures and rules imposed by the federal government. Possessing knowledge of the federal procurement system goes a long way toward improving the chances of winning and successfully performing government contracts. Understanding the human dimensions of life can take the enlightened contractor even further.

I have learned over the years that *"people buy from people,"* and that *"the government doesn't buy, people do."* The federal government has excellent, dedicated people, but they are understaffed, overworked, under-trained, under-supported and, unfortunately, under-valued. Consequently, government program managers depend on contractors to assist. Thus, contractor selection is a critical decision, and the decision is usually based on human considerations and on a strong relationship of trust with contractors.

The massive size of the federal government may give the impression that it's an impenetrable bureaucracy. Yet at its core, federal contracting is fundamentally a *people-to-people* business.

As federal rules governing contract awards have continuously changed and become more complex over the years, it has also become increasingly difficult for small business facilitators like the Offices of Small and Disadvantaged Business Utilization (OSDBUs) to allocate equal time to the many firms that approach them. Therefore, there's a discussion they deliver to the *masses* and another one they reserve for *individuals*. Ask yourself which one you are and what your **"competitiveness discriminators"** are to enable you to command special attention.

Here's a *"gem of wisdom:"* Anyone can be a small business owner, but not everyone is an entrepreneur. In my opinion, entrepreneurship requires knowledge, confidence, capability, and the **ability to inspire others**. It's the latter portion of the formula that is particularly important. Entrepreneurship is a state of mind; it's a will to adventure and push the envelope. Clearly, all small business owners develop some of these traits, but having a true entrepreneurial spirit is to possess that special X factor that enables you to command attention.

Here's another "gem of wisdom:" Since the federal government buys repeatable goods and services, look at existing suppliers and develop similar profiles. When I was on the federal side, I would describe companies as *bodies* with interchangeable *heads*. The *body* is the core of expertise with past performance, and the *head* is the new owner. New owners (*heads*) come into the game looking for the existing expertise (*bodies*) that they need to acquire. Such is the circle of life in federal contracting!

I have had the good fortune of being on both sides of the government contracting fence.

It all started in 1973, when I began my federal government career. During my tenure with the federal government, I served as a Contracting Officer, Procurement Analyst, a *Procurement Center Representative (PCR)* for the U.S. Small Business Administration (SBA), and as *Director of Small Business Programs* at the Office of the Secretary, U.S. Department of Health and Human Services (HHS) for over 10 years. As a procurement professional, I developed a deep understanding of how the federal government works.

After retiring from the federal government in the latter part of 2000, I capitalized on the institutional knowledge I gained while serving in the government and leveraged it—*in the true spirit of entrepreneurship*—and started my own business as a federal contractor in the 8(a)BD program.

Over a six-year period, my firm grew from just 4 employees to over 300 employees at its peak, during which time it earned recognition for its achievements at the national, state, and local levels. It was ranked #2 in *2005 on Washington Technology's "Fast 50" list of Government Contractors;* it ranked #90 on *Black Enterprise Magazine's "2006 BE 100;" it was awarded the 2006 Tech Council of Maryland (TCM) prestigious "Government Contracting Firm of the Year" award;* and was selected as *Montgomery County Chamber of Commerce's "2006 Emerging Business of the Year."*

In 2007, I beat my own odds: I sold my business in six years rather than in the ten I had planned.

For me, learning the art of "hearing and adhering" to the desires of federal government end users was the key to success. When I paid attention and listened to them, they helped me. Specifically, they assisted me in identifying opportunities and directing me to information and contacts that helped me capture the opportunities.

And here's my last *"gem of wisdom:"* Never think about marketing to "the federal government." The market needs to be broken down into logical segments that can be dealt with one segment at a time. How do you eat an elephant? *One bite at a time.*

Verl Zanders
Entrepreneur

How to Order Books By AASBEA Publishers

By Credit Card: WWW.AASBEA.COM **PayPal** ADD TO CART

By Direct Purchase: Mail check ($19.99 + $5.00 S&H) to:
AASBEA Publishers
2300 M Street, NW, Suite 800
Washington, DC 20037
Email: info@aasbea.com
Web: www.aasbea.com

By "Special Order" at all Major Bookstores, cite: **ISBN 978-0-9816885-0-3**

Books by AASBEA Publishers:

- *Gems of Wisdom for Succeeding in the 8(a) BD Program & Beyond* (Freeman, S.T., & Kruvant, M.C., 2007)

- *African Americans Reviving Baseball in Inner Cities* (Freeman, S.T., 2008)

- *Africa's Youth Define Leadership* (Freeman, S.T., & Walker, W.A., 2007)

- *How To Sell Into The U.S. Market From Pakistan: A Practical "How To" Guide for SMEs* (Freeman, S. T., 2006)

- *African Leaders Reach Out to Africans in the Diaspora* (Freeman, S.T., 2004)

- *Making It In America: Conversations With Successful Ethiopian American Entrepreneurs* (Gebre, P.H., 2004)

- *Conversations With Powerful African Women Leaders: Inspiration, Motivation, and Strategy* (Freeman, S.T., 2002)

- *Recipes From the Road: Favorite Global Recipes of Washington, DC's Global Women* (Freeman, S.T., 2002)

- *Exporting, Importing, and E-Commerce: A "How To" Guide For Minority, Immigrant, and Women-Owned Firms* (Freeman, S.T., 2001)

- *Conversations With Women Who Export: Inspiration, Motivation, and Strategy* (Freeman, S.T., 2000)

Some Also Available on Amazon.com

Acknowledgments

O n behalf of all current and former 8(a)BD firms, deep gratitude is expressed to all supporters in and outside of the federal government who have given these firms a chance to demonstrate their competence and to make a valuable contribution toward helping the government achieve its objectives.

As the saying goes, "It takes a village…," and there are many in the village of supporters of the 8(a)BD program and its firms. Thank you one and all, and special thanks to all who shared their *Gems of Wisdom* for this book.

About Author

Dr. Sharon T. Freeman

Dr. Freeman is a community and small business development advocate and International and Development Specialist who has worked in over 100 countries and has written and published numerous books on related subjects. She advises foreign governments, multinational corporations, small businesses, minority, immigrant, and women-owned businesses on how to thrive in an increasingly competitive global marketplace. She formerly served in the U.S. Diplomatic Corps and resided and worked in Hong Kong for 12 years. She is an Advisor to U.S. Secretary of Commerce and U.S. Trade Representative on *Trade Policy Matters Affecting Small Business*. She is also a member of the Advisory Boards of the U.S. Trade Representative's *Trade Advisory Committee on Africa* and the U.S. Department of Energy's Small Business Advisory Board. She formerly served as a two-term member the U.S. Export Import Bank's Advisory Board, as the Chair of the DC Chamber's International Committee, and as the Director of the DC Government's International Business Development Office.

Dr. Freeman began her international consulting career with Booz, Allen & Hamilton, and subsequently worked for the U.S. Government in various senior positions in organizations involved in trade and development. She formed the Lark-Horton consulting practice in Hong Kong in 1985.

In addition to serving as the President and CEO of the Lark-Horton firm, Dr. Freeman also serves as the Founder and President of two other firms: The All American Business Exporters Association (AASBEA), publisher of this book, which is dedicated exclusively to facilitating the participation of minority, immigrant, and women-owned firms in global and e-commerce marketplaces, and the International Foundation for Trade and Investment Skills Development, a 501 (c) (3) non profit.

Dr. Freeman holds a Ph.D. in Applied Management and Decision Sciences from Walden University (1998), and was recognized as the Walden University *Alumna of the Year 2006* (*see video clip at: http://realpeople.waldenu.edu/video-sharon.cfm*). She also holds a Masters of Science from Carnegie-Mellon University in Public Policy and Management (1977), and dual Bachelor of Arts degrees from Carnegie Mellon in Cognitive Psychology and History (1974).

About Author

Charito Kruvant

M. Charito Kruvant is President and CEO of Creative Associates International, Inc. a 28-year-old professional services firm that builds capacity for education, civil society, communities in transition, elections and political processes, and security and stabilization, among many other efforts.

Charito is the Chair of the Board of Trustees of The Community Foundation for the National Capital Region. She also chairs several organizations and is a member of the Board of Directors of Acacia Federal Savings Bank and Calvert Funds for socially responsible investing. She is also a member of the board of the Summit Fund of Washington and member of the executive and grants committees of the Venture Philanthropy Partners.

Charito has received numerous awards. Born in Bolivia and raised in Argentina, she received a Bachelor of Arts from Colegio Ward in Argentina and a Master of Arts in Early Childhood Development from the University of Maryland. She has been a resident of the Washington, DC area for more than 30 years.

Known for her advocacy on behalf of small businesses and for community contributions, she formerly chaired the U.S. Small Business Administration's (SBA) Washington Metropolitan Area District Advisory Council and served on its District of Columbia Geographical Trade Area Subcommittee. As Committee Chair she led the Advisory Council in advising and making recommendations to the SBA on the effectiveness of existing programs and services and in serving as a link to the local business community and to other public and private sector organizations.

Charito understands the value of the 8(a)BD program. Today, though extremely busy as the CEO of the firm she started while in the program, she is never too busy to share her own personal *"Gems of Wisdom"* with 8(a)BD firms to help them increase their competitiveness.

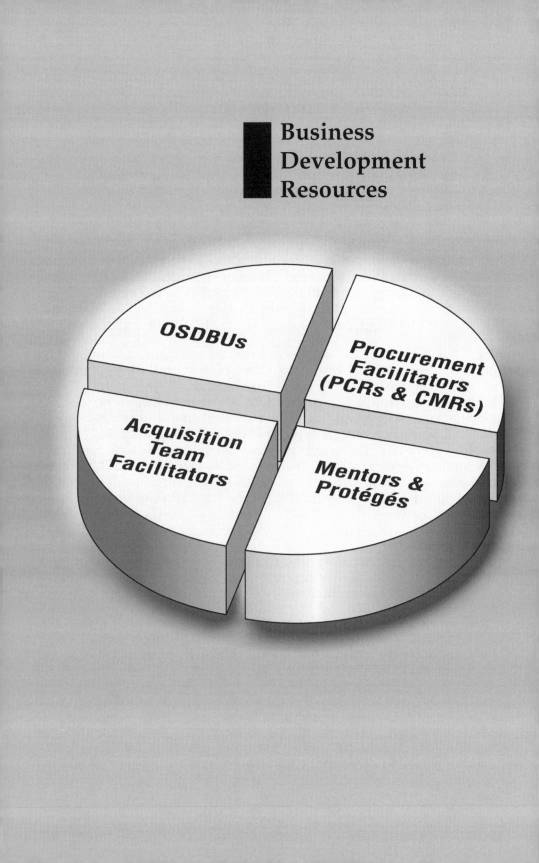

Business Development Resources

OSDBUs

Procurement Facilitators (PCRs & CMRs)

Acquisition Team Facilitators

Mentors & Protégés

Introduction

The federal marketplace is no longer national; it is international. International trade agreements between the United States and other countries have facilitated this transformation. Consequently, companies are in a never-ending quest to stand apart from the competition.

This book is part of a series of *Gems of Wisdom* books that provide business development assistance to 8(a)BD firms. Whereas the first book in the series provided advice of successful 8(a)BD graduates about how to succeed in the program and *beyond*, this book aims to increase the competitiveness of 8(a)BD firms by sharing *gems of wisdom* of those in the field who are active participants in and facilitators of the program.

The 8(a) Business Development program, hereinafter referred to as 8(a)BD, is designed to provide business development assistance and technical assistance to help socially and economically disadvantaged American businesses gain access to the mainstream American economy. The program is named for the section of the Small Business Act that authorizes its policies and procedures.

This book shines a spotlight on the network of resources that are provided to help 8(a)BD firms develop their business and increase their competitiveness. These resources include, but are not limited to, Offices of Small and Disadvantaged Business Utilization (OSDBUs), procurement facilitators such as Procurement Center Representatives (PCRs), Commercial Marketing Representatives (CMRs), acquisition team members such as contract and program offices, and mentors. This book provides insights into how to utilize these resources and imparts a deeper understanding of how they fit together in a comprehensive business development network.

8(a)BD firm owners that read this book should walk away with an in-depth understanding of where to go for business development assistance and how to optimize the utilization of resources in their efforts to develop their businesses and to take maximum advantage of available assistance.

They should also walk away with a renewed understanding of why certain resources have been made available, what level of assistance is provided through these resources, and how they should use them to their best advantage in increasing their competitiveness. Importantly, this book is intended to demonstrate that there are no shortcuts or substitutes for learning how the federal system within which the 8(a)BD program operates works.

To take maximum advantage of the *"hand up"* the 8(a) certification and its business development program offers, it's incumbent upon firm owners to maximize their understanding of the federal government contracting environment. Firm owners don't have to learn this on their own, however. There are many resources out there to help them. Some of the key resources are discussed herein.

This book is organized in four chapters. The first focuses on the role of the OSDBUs in helping 8(a)BD firms increase their competitiveness. The second focuses on the role of procurement facilitators, such as PCRs and CMRs. The third focuses on the role of various acquisition team members, such as Contract Officers, Contract Officer Technical Representatives (COTRs), and Program Officers, and the fourth focuses on Mentors and Protégés in the 8(a)BD program. There is a reason why this book is organized in this way. Essentially, the aforementioned entities are part of what can be considered as "the expanded business development team" that is in place to help 8(a)BD firms succeed. Whereas Business Opportunity Specialists (BOSs) are the first in the line of those that offer business development assistance to 8(a)BD firms, it's equally important to effectively utilize resources that are available from the broader business development network.

It's useful to step back and reflect on how these entities came into being and what their purposes are. Accordingly, a reminder is given in the overview below.

Federal Contracting With Small and Disadvantaged Businesses: An Historical Perspective

> *"Public Law 95-507 has been heralded as the most comprehensive statute ever enacted dealing with minority business development."*

How did we get there and where are we now?

It started with the government's interest in promoting small businesses, which initially emerged in response to the nation's economic pressures during the Great Depression and World War II. In 1932 President Herbert Hoover created the Reconstruction Finance Corporation (RFC), a lending program for large and small businesses hurt by the depression.

During World War II, small businesses suffered as large businesses stepped up production to accommodate wartime demands. In response, Congress created the Smaller War Plans Corporation in 1942 to provide direct loans to private entrepreneurs and promote small businesses to federal procurement agencies. The Corporation dissolved after the war, and its responsibilities were turned over to RFC and the Office of Small Business in the Department of Commerce, which primarily provided educational services and conducted management counseling for entrepreneurs.

In 1952, in response to efforts to abolish the RFC, President Dwight D. Eisenhower proposed the creation of the **Small Business Administration (SBA)** to consolidate the government's fragmented small business programs. Congress codified the proposal by passing the Small Business Act of 1953, directing SBA to "aid, counsel, assist and protect" small business concerns. SBA immediately began making direct loans and guaranteeing bank loans to small businesses, working to open federal procurement to such firms, and providing technical assistance and training.

The Small Business Act of 1958 authorized SBA to enter into agreements with other federal agencies for the purpose of granting subcontracts to small businesses. In 1969, SBA modified its regulations to direct federal procurement contracts specifically to minority-owned small businesses. Congress statutorily authorized this change with the 1978 amendments to the Small Business Act and Small Business Investment Act of 1958.

The **1978 act** required federal agencies to ensure that small businesses owned and controlled by socially and economically disadvantaged individuals (known as small disadvantaged businesses, or SDBs) have maximum opportunity to participate in federal contracts.

The Small Business Act defines socially disadvantaged individuals as those who belong to groups that have been subject to racial or ethnic discrimination or cultural bias. It defines economically disadvantaged individuals as those whose ability to compete has been compromised by diminished credit and capital opportunities compared to those who are not disadvantaged. To improve opportunities, Congress later established an annual goal for participation of small disadvantaged businesses at 5 percent of the total value of all prime contract and subcontract awards. Each federal agency is also required to establish its own goals.

To participate as an SBA-certified small disadvantaged business (SDB) a business must be "small" as defined in SBA regulations, and 51 percent owned by individuals who qualify as economically disadvantaged. The SBA presumes that Blacks, Hispanics, Asian Pacific Americans, Subcontinent Asians, and Native Americans, as well as members of other groups designated from time to time, are socially disadvantaged. It also allows individuals who are not members of these groups to assert social disadvantage based on evidence. In addition, all program participants must prove economic disadvantage according to criteria established in agency regulations.

The **1978 Small Business Act** also established **Offices of Small and Disadvantaged Business Utilization (OSDBUs)** and gave them procurement powers at each federal agency. The Act charges each agency's OSDBU director with promoting the interests of small and disadvantaged businesses pursuing federal contracts. The legislation assigns several specific responsibilities to OSDBUs, including overseeing contracts to ensure that small businesses have the maximum practicable opportunity to participate as prime and subcontractors, providing assistance and information for firms preparing contract bids, and ensuring timely payment of contractors. OSDBU staff consult with SBA to implement these responsibilities.

> Among the responsibilities with which the OSDBUs are charged, some of the most important are overseeing contracts to ensure that small businesses have the maximum practicable opportunity to participate as prime and subcontractors and providing assistance and information for firms preparing contract bids. These responsibilities will be discussed at length in subsequent chapters.

Other legislative and regulatory actions over the years established programs that similarly helped small disadvantaged businesses compete with larger and non-disadvantaged enterprises. The **Federal Acquisition Streamlining Act of 1994** (FASA), for instance, authorized all federal agencies to offer race-conscious procurement to meet SDB participation goals pursuant to the Small Business Act, and reemphasized the flexible 5 percent target.

Incrementally, between 1968 and 1998, federal agencies and Congress recognized the need for measures to make contracting opportunities more accessible to minority-owned firms and economically disadvantaged businesses. Significant within the resulting statutory framework was:

- **SBA's 8(a) Business Development Program**, named for the section of law that implemented it, acknowledges that certain businesses lack key resources to successfully compete for contracts, and offers SDBs assistance. The program promotes development through a wide range of mechanisms over a nine-year period (unless a business should graduate early).

- The **8(a) Business Development Mentor-Protégé Program**, which was finalized in 1998, allows businesses participating in the 8(a) program to receive assistance from a successful business, which acts as the mentor. Both mentor and protégé can cooperate in competing for federal procurement and accessing capital in the form of equity loans.

Qualifying for eligibility became somewhat more rigorous, however, with **post-***Adarand* requirements for businesses to obtain formal certification to participate.

Federal Contracting After *Adarand*

Thirty years after the Civil Rights Act of 1964, and subsequent executive orders prohibiting hiring discrimination by federal contractors and requiring businesses to provide affirmative action plans with large bids, the Supreme Court's 1995 decision in *Adarand Constructors, Inc. v.Peña* (*Adarand*) clarified the constitutional standard for evaluating race-conscious programs in federal contracting. The Court held that all racial classifications imposed by federal, state, or local governments must be subjected to "strict scrutiny," a standard used by the courts in deciding whether a law or policy is constitutional.

In 1995, the *Adarand* decision prompted federal agencies to reevaluate contracting practices. The specific contract in question resulted from the Surface Transportation and Uniform Relocation Assistance Act of 1987, which mandated that at least 10 percent of DOT funds be expended with SDBs (or disadvantaged business enterprises—DBEs—as they are known in transportation procurement), using the same definitions of social and economic disadvantage found in the Small Business Act.

Agency regulations in place at the time of the legal challenge stated that a contract applicant should be *presumed* both socially and economically disadvantaged, and thus eligible for the program, if the applicant belonged to a certain racial group. As with DOT, most federal contracts contained a subcontractor compensation clause, which gave prime contractors financial incentive to hire SDB-certified subcontractors. Adarand filed suit against federal officials claiming that the race-based presumption of disadvantage violated the Fifth Amendment's Due Process Clause, which courts have interpreted to require equal enforcement of the laws.

After the *Adarand* decision, federal agencies reexamined contracting procedures and began to alter disadvantaged business programs. DOT had already begun to modify its SDB contracting program. When the lower court reviewed the case again, it determined that DOT's program did not meet the strict scrutiny standard. During the appeals process, DOT altered the definition of "disadvantaged businesses" to include socially and economically disadvantaged firms, in addition to those challenged by discrimination, regardless of race. The new Disadvantaged Business Enterprise (DBE) program, DOT asserted, is open to "everyone, regardless of race or ethnicity, who meets the statutory criteria for social and economic disadvantage based on individual experience.

In 1999, DOT issued new regulations that significantly altered the program in response to *Adarand*. The regulations designated 10 percent as a national *aspirational* goal for disadvantaged businesses, *but mandated actual participation goals at levels based on the local market availability of DBEs, not a set percentage*. Moreover, the regulations required states to use race-neutral measures, including outreach and technical assistance, to meet as much of their goals as possible. Other agencies similarly revised their SDB programs. They focused largely on the narrow tailoring requirement, relying on six factors the courts identified to assess whether a program complies:

(1) Whether race-neutral alternatives were first considered and determined to be insufficient solutions;

(2) The scope of the program and whether it is flexible;

(3) Whether race is the sole factor in eligibility or one factor among others;

(4) Whether any numerical target is reasonably related to the number of qualified minorities in the applicant pool;

(5 Whether the duration of the program is limited and subject to periodic review; and

6) The extent of the burden imposed on non-beneficiaries of the program.

The foregoing demonstrates that the legal and regulatory framework within which the 8(a)BD program exists is dynamic. Nothing can be taken for granted and things do not necessarily stay the same.

While it's not possible to predict the future, there are good reasons to understand the past because understanding it equips firms with the knowledge they need to more effectively utilize resources. When firm owners understand the big picture they can operate more effectively. Accordingly, a snapshot of the aforementioned legislation and regulations that affects federal prime contracts and subcontracts is presented below. It is taken from a September 2006 U.S. Small Business Administration, Office of Advocacy report that examined the government's role in aiding small businesses in subcontracting.

Selected Legislation and Regulations Affecting Federal Prime Contracts and Subcontracts

Year	Legislation/ Regulation	Description
1958	Public Law 85-536	This legislation amended the Small Business Act of 1953 and authorized a voluntary subcontracting program. Prior to 1978, this statute was implemented most effectively in the Armed Services Procurement Regulations (ASPR), a predecessor to the FAR. It required large contractors receiving contracts over $500,000 with substantial subcontracting opportunities to establish a program that would enable minority business concerns to be considered fairly as subcontractors or suppliers.
1978	Public Law 95-507	This legislation amended Section 8(d) of the Small Business Act and created the foundation for the Subcontracting Assistance Program. Section 211 of Public Law 95-507 is the same as 8(d), as it is known today. It changed the participation of large contractors in the program from voluntary to mandatory, and it changed the language of the law from "best efforts" to "maximum practicable opportunities." Key features include: (a) a requirement that all federal contracts in excess of $100,000 (as amended) provide maximum practicable opportunity for small and small disadvantaged businesses to participate; and (b) a requirement that all federal contracts in excess of $500,000 ($1,000,000 in the case of construction contracts for public facilities) is accompanied by a formal subcontracting plan containing separate goals for small business and small disadvantaged business.
1984	Public Law 98-577	The Small Business and Federal Procurement Act of 1984. This legislation amended the Small Business Act as follows: (a) by providing that small and small disadvantaged businesses be given the maximum practicable opportunity to participate in contracts and subcontracts for subsystems, assemblies, components, and related services for major systems; and (b) by requiring federal agencies to establish procedures to ensure the timely payment of amounts due pursuant to the terms of their subcontracts with small and small disadvantaged businesses.
1987	Public Law 99-661	The National Defense Authorization Act of 1987. Section 1207 of this statute required the Department of Defense to establish as its objective a goal of five percent of the total combined amount obligated for contracts and subcontracts entered into with small and small disadvantaged businesses in each of fiscal years 1987, 1988, and 1989. Also, the use of SDB set-asides was authorized. (Subsequent legislation extended this period through the year 2000; however, the set-aside aspect of the program was suspended in fiscal year 1996.)
1988	Public Law 100-180	Section 806 required the secretary of defense to increase awards to small and small disadvantaged businesses.
1988	Public Law 100-656	The principal focus of this legislation was the 8(a) Program, but it contained a number of other provisions which affected the Subcontracting Assistance Program. These other provisions included the following: (a) Section 304 requires that the FAR be amended to include a requirement for a contract clause authorizing the government to assess liquidated damages against large contractors which fail to perform according to the terms of their subcontracting plans and cannot demonstrate that they have made a good faith effort to do so; (b) Section 502, now codified at 15 U.S.C. Section 644(g)(1), requires the president to establish annual goals for procurement contracts of not less than 20 percent for small business prime contract awards and not less than 5 percent for small disadvantaged business prime contract and subcontract awards for each fiscal year [emphasis added]; and, (c) Section 503 requires the SBA to compile

Year	Legislation/Regulation	Description
		and analyze reports each year submitted by individual agencies to assess their success in attaining government-wide goals for small and small disadvantaged businesses, and to submit the report to the president.
1990	Public Law 101-189	Defense Authorization Act. Section 834 established the Test Program for the Negotiation of Comprehensive Subcontracting Plans. This statute authorized a pilot program limited to a few Department of Defense large contractors approved by the Office of Small and Disadvantaged Business Utilization (OSDBU) at the Pentagon. The program allows these companies to have one company-wide subcontracting plan for all defense contracts, rather than individual subcontracting plans for every contract over $500,000, and it waives the requirement for the semi-annual SF 294 *Subcontracting Report for Individual Contracts*. The large contractor is still required to submit the SF 295 semi-annually, and it is required to have individual subcontracting plans and to submit SF 294s on any contracts with other government agencies. Public Law 103-355, Section 7103, extended this test program through September 30, 1998.
1990/1	Public Law 101-510	The National Defense Authorization Act for Fiscal Year 1991. Section 831 established the Pilot Mentor Protégé Program to encourage assistance to small disadvantaged businesses through special incentives to companies approved as mentors. The government reimburses the mentor for the cost of assistance to its protégés, or, as an alternative, allows the mentor credit (a multiple of the dollars in assistance) toward subcontracting goals. Prior to receiving reimbursement or credit, mentors must submit formal applications.
1992	Public Law 102-366	The Small Business Credit and Business Opportunity Enhancement Act. Section 232(a) (6) removes the requirement from SBA to do the Annual Report to Congress on Unacceptable Subcontracting Plans, which had been found in Section 8(d) of the Small Business Act.
1994	Public Law 103-355	The Federal Acquisition Streamlining Act. FASA significantly simplifies and streamlines the federal procurement process. Section 7106 of FASA revised Sections 8 and 15 of the Small Business Act to establish a government-wide goal of 5 percent participation by women-owned small businesses, in both prime and subcontracts. Women-owned small businesses are to be given equal standing with small and small disadvantaged business in subcontracting plans. In practical terms, this means that all subcontracting plans after October 1, 1995, must contain goals for women-owned small businesses and that all FAR references to small and small disadvantaged business have been changed to small, small disadvantaged, and women-owned small business.
1997	Public Law 105-135	The HUBZone Empowerment Contracting Program, which is included in the Small Business Reauthorization Act of 1997, stimulates economic development and creates jobs in urban and rural communities by providing contracting preferences to small businesses that are located in HUBZones and hire employees who live in HUBZones.
1999	Public Law 106-50	The Veterans Entrepreneurship and Small Business Development Act. This established a goal for subcontracts awarded by prime contractors to service-disabled veteran-owned small business concerns of 3 percent. A best effort goal will be established for veteran-owned small businesses. Subcontracting plans must incorporate these goals.
	FAR Part 19 (48 CFR)	Implements the procurement sections of the Small Business Act. Federal contracting agencies must conduct their acquisitions in compliance with these regulations. OTSB contractors are required to comply with certain clauses and provisions referenced in the FAR. These are: (a) Subpart 19.1 prescribes policies and procedures for size standards (also in Title 13 of the U.S. Code of Federal

Small Business Goaling *Today*

Whatever changes might occur in the legal and regulatory framework, "the show must go on." One of the key parts played is by the U.S. Small Business Administration (SBA), which is responsible for the management and oversight of the small business procurement process across the federal government. SBA negotiates with federal departments concerning their prime contracting goals and achievement with small businesses to ensure that small businesses have the maximum practicable opportunity to provide goods and services to the Federal government.

Negotiations ensure that the federal government will achieve not less than 23 percent to small businesses. Statutory goals have been established for Federal executive agencies. They are:

- 23 percent of prime contracts for small businesses;
- 5 percent of prime and subcontracts for small disadvantaged businesses, including 8(a)s;
- 5 percent of prime and subcontracts for women-owned small businesses;
- 3 percent of prime contracts for HUBZone small businesses;
- 3 percent of prime and subcontracts for service-disabled veteran-owned small businesses.

In addition to the goals established, the Small Business Act 15(g)(1) also states that it is the policy of the United States, that each agency shall have an annual goal that represents, for that agency, the maximum practicable opportunity for small business concerns, small business concerns owned and controlled by service disabled veterans, qualified HUBZone small business concerns, small business concerns owned and operated by socially and economically disadvantaged individuals, and small business concerns owned and controlled by women to participate in the performance of contracts let by that agency

The *Small Business Goaling Report* documents the achievement by each department, and the Small Business Procurement Scorecards provide an assessment of federal achievement in prime contracting to small businesses by the twenty-four Chief Financial Officers Act agencies. It also measures progress that departments are making to ensure small business opportunities remain an integral part of their acquisition of goods and services to meet mission objectives. The scorecard was designed as an internal control and monitoring device to ensure that (1) Federal agencies reach their small business and socio-economic goals, (2) accurate and transparent contracting data is used and (3) agency-specific progress is maintained. SBA issues the *Small Business Procurement Scorecards* in alliance with the President's Management Agenda.

Monitoring Achievements Towards Goals

The SBA uses the procurement data in the **Federal Procurement Data System (FPDS)** to monitor agencies' achievements against goals. The FPDS is the official Federal procurement data source. Agencies report each award over $25,000 separately with details about that award such as; industry, place of performance, type of contractor, if the contractor meets SBA's size standards, and amount. Awards under $25,000 are also reported, but in summary form that does not include specific details about each small purchase. The agencies' prime contractors, who win awards over $500,000 ($1 million if construction), also report on their subcontracting to small business by goal category. SBA monitors the agencies' performance throughout the year using the FPDS data and compares the agencies' achievements with its goals.

Reporting Achievements and Goals

When the mid-year data are available, SBA reports to each major federal procurement agency on their progress towards goals for that fiscal year. SBA also prepares an annual report for the President that shows government-wide and agency specific performance. It's available on SBA's web site at *(http://www.sba.gov/gc/goals)*, along with other useful information pertaining to contracting with the federal government. Federal small business prime contracting goals for FY 2007 are shown in Table 1 on the following page. They can also be retrieved from SBA at: *http://www.sba.gov/aboutsba/sbaprograms/goals/fy2007/index.html*.

Federal Government Contract Overview

Goals are one thing getting a piece of the "gold" is another. To get in the game and to win, 8(a)BD firms must master the rules of federal government contracting, and that's not easy. "In order to succeed in the 8(a)BD program participants must learn the rules of government contracting," according to successful 8(a)BD graduates.

Successful 8(a)BD graduates also emphasize that in addition to developing their firm's product and service offerings, they had to master the process of contracting with the federal government in order to succeed. At the same time, their advice underscores that there's a lot to learn about operating in the federal marketplace. No one masters the information overnight or without help. Successful firms take time, commit resources, and engage partners, as needed, to incrementally enhance their ability to successfully compete in the government and commercial marketplaces.

Table 1. Fiscal Year 2007: Federal Small Business Prime Contracting Goals

Agency	Small Business	8(A)	Sdb	Women	Hubzone	Service Disabled Veteran
Executive Office of the President	50.00%	15.00%	25.00%	9.00%	3.00%	3.00%
Department of Agriculture	49.00%	5.00%	5.00%	5.00%	5.50%	3.00%
Department of Commerce	48.00%	6.11%	12.00%	8.50%	3.00%	3.00%
Department of Defense	23.00%	2.60%	3.20%	5.00%	3.00%	3.00%
Department of Education	23.00%	4.00%	5.00%	5.00%	3.00%	3.00%
Department of Energy	4.42%	1.22%	1.69%	0.39%	0.11%	0.08%
Department of Health and Human Services	30.32%	5.50%	5.50%	5.05%	3.03%	3.00%
Department of Homeland Security	30.00%	4.00%	4.00%	5.00%	3.00%	3.00%
Department of Housing and Urban Development	45.00%	10.00%	10.00%	20.00%	3.50%	3.00%
Department of Justice	32.42%	3.00%	5.50%	5.00%	3.00%	3.00%
Department of Labor	26.00%	4.84%	5.20%	5.20%	3.00%	3.00%
Department of State	36.00%	3.00%	7.00%	5.00%	3.00%	3.00%
Department of the Interior	56.14%	8.26%	10.83%	6.66%	6.00%	3.00%
Department of the Treasury	26.00%	5.00%	6.00%	6.00%	3.00%	3.00%
Department of Transportation	35.31%	7.00%	7.00%	5.00%	3.00%	3.00%
Department of Veterans Affairs	27.77%	5.00%	9.00%	5.00%	3.05%	3.00%
Agency for International Development	23.00%	2.50%	5.00%	5.00%	3.00%	3.00%
American Battle Monuments Commission	23.00%	2.50%	2.50%	5.00%	3.00%	3.00%
Broadcasting Board of Governors	37.42%	3.73%	4.74%	5.00%	3.00%	3.00%
Commodity Futures Trading Commission	22.96%	2.50%	2.50%	5.00%	3.00%	3.00%
Consumer Product Safety Commission	48.00%	9.98%	19.99%	12.98%	3.00%	3.00%
Court Services and Offender	23.00%	2.50%	2.50%	5.00%	3.00%	3.00%
Defense Nuclear Facilities Services	23.00%	2.50%	2.50%	5.00%	3.00%	3.00%
Environmental Protection Agency	36.00%	7.50%	3.00%	5.50%	3.00%	3.00%
Equal Employment Opportunity	38.00%	5.00%	6.00%	5.00%	3.00%	3.00%
Export-import Bank of The U. S.	23.00%	2.50%	2.50%	5.00%	3.00%	3.00%
Farm Credit Administration	23.00%	2.50%	2.50%	5.00%	3.00%	3.00%
Federal Communications Commission	23.00%	2.50%	2.50%	5.00%	3.00%	3.00%
Federal Election Commission	31.52%	2.50%	2.50%	5.00%	3.00%	3.00%
Federal Energy Regulatory Commission	23.00%	2.50%	2.50%	5.00%	3.00%	3.00%
Federal Labor Relations Authority	23.00%	2.50%	2.50%	5.00%	3.00%	3.00%
Federal Maritime Commission	23.00%	2.50%	2.50%	5.00%	3.00%	3.00%
Federal Mediation and Council	23.00%	2.50%	2.50%	5.00%	3.00%	3.00%
Federal Trade Commission	23.00%	2.50%	2.50%	5.00%	3.00%	3.00%
General Services Administration	45.00%	5.00%	8.00%	5.00%	3.00%	3.00%
International Trade Commission	23.00%	2.50%	2.50%	5.00%	3.00%	3.00%
J. F. Kennedy Center for The Arts	23.00%	2.50%	2.50%	5.00%	3.00%	3.00%
Merit Systems Protection Board	42.66%	2.50%	2.50%	5.00%	3.00%	3.00%
Millenium Challenge Corporation	23.00%	2.50%	5.00%	5.00%	3.00%	3.00%
National Aeronautics and Space Administration	16.16%	4.05%	6.50%	5.00%	3.00%	3.00%
National Archives and Record	31.00%	3.20%	5.00%	5.00%	3.00%	3.00%
National Endowment for the Arts	23.00%	14.66%	2.00%	5.00%	3.00%	14.66%
National Endowment for the Humanities	23.00%	2.50%	2.50%	5.00%	3.00%	3.00%
National Gallery of Art	23.00%	2.50%	2.50%	5.00%	3.00%	3.00%
National Labor Relations Board	23.00%	2.50%	2.50%	5.00%	3.00%	3.00%
National Mediation Board	23.00%	2.50%	2.50%	5.00%	3.00%	3.00%
National Science Foundation	23.00%	2.50%	2.50%	5.00%	3.00%	3.00%
National Transportation Safety Board	23.00%	2.50%	2.50%	5.00%	3.00%	3.00%
Nuclear Regulatory Commission	32.73%	4.00%	5.40%	7.45%	3.00%	3.00%
Office of Personnel Management	23.00%	2.20%	5.00%	10.38%	3.00%	3.00%
Peace Corps	25.00%	4.00%	2.50%	5.00%	3.00%	3.00%
Railroad Retirement Board	29.30%	1.60%	5.40%	5.50%	3.00%	4.20%
Securities and Exchange Commission	23.00%	2.50%	5.00%	5.00%	3.00%	3.00%
Selective Service System	23.00%	2.50%	2.50%	5.00%	3.00%	3.00%
Small Business Administration	60.00%	20.00%	36.00%	10.00%	3.00%	3.00%
Smithsonian Institution	50.00%	6.66%	6.66%	5.00%	3.00%	3.00%
Social Security Administration	33.82%	8.50%	12.47%	5.00%	3.00%	3.00%
United States Holocaust Memorial	23.00%	2.50%	2.50%	5.00%	3.00%	3.00%
United States Soldiers and Airmans Home	23.00%	2.50%	2.50%	5.00%	3.00%	3.00%
United States Trade and Development	50.64%	7.60%	13.97%	5.00%	3.00%	2.54%
Statutory (Or SBA Assigned Goals)	**23.00%**	**2.50%**	**2.50%**	**5.00%**	**3.00%**	**3.00%**

Graduates also underscore that while the 8(a)BD program is an important socio-economic program for which the U.S. Government imposes obligations in the contracting process, it is only a hand up; not a hand out. Importantly, it doesn't exempt any of its recipients from the necessity of having to learn the rules of contracting with the federal government.

Contracting with the federal government is a highly regulated process. Unlike commercial contracting, which is governed generally by the Uniform Commercial Code and common law, federal government contracting is governed by various statutes and regulations. These statutory and regulatory provisions dictate, for example, what method or process agencies must use to solicit contracts; how agencies must negotiate or award contracts; and under certain circumstances, what costs the government will reimburse and how contractors must account for those costs. Although Congress has streamlined the contracting process to reduce the burden on contractors offering commercial products and services, any entity, including 8(a)BD firms, considering entering into a government contract must understand the rules.

Government contracting officials use procedures that conform to the Federal Acquisition Regulations (FAR). Learning how the government buys, understanding the responsibilities of contractors and recognizing subcontracting and procurement opportunities are the first steps to navigating the complex world of contracting.

The SBA provides a wealth of information to help 8(a)BD firms learn about contracting with the federal government. Information, which is also available on SBA's website, is presented below.

Defining the Market

Selling to the federal government is, in some ways, similar to selling to the private sector. While federal procurement procedures may have a different set of rules and regulations, many of the same marketing techniques used in the private sector may apply. For instance, in any situation one must use common business sense. It's common sense to get to know the agency and understand the context in which your product or service could be used.

Obtain available information on past awards, quantities, costs and awarders. Become known to potential purchasers. Before going forward, take a moment to think about your company's products and services. Take a close look at your company and consider what the government will look for when considering your company for a contract award. In addition to past performance, financial status, staff capabilities and track record are all of interest to the government.

How the Government Buys

The government buys many of the products and services it needs from suppliers who meet certain qualifications. It applies standardized procedures by which to purchase goods and services and uses procedures that conform to the Federal Acquisition Regulation (FAR).

The FAR is a standardized set of regulations used by all federal agencies in making purchases. It provides procedures for every step in the procurement process, from the time someone in the government discovers a need for a product or service to the time the purchase is complete. The FAR can be accessed electronically at *www.arnet.gov/far*.

As of October 1, 2001, the government transitioned from Commerce Business Daily (CBD) to Federal Business Opportunities (**FedBizOpps**) to "post" all procurement opportunities expected to exceed $25,000. FedBizOpps is a web-based application and is the government-wide point of entry to communicate its buying requirements to potential suppliers. This very important website can be accessed at *www.FedBizOpps.gov*.

When the government wants to purchase a certain product or service, it can use a variety of contracting methods. Simplified acquisition procedures, sealed bidding, contracting by negotiation and consolidated purchasing vehicles are key contract methodologies used to purchase products and services.

Contracting Methods

The Federal Acquisition Streamlining Act (FASA) of 1994 is intended to simplify government buying procedures. It removed many competition restrictions on government purchases of less than $100,000. Instead of full and open competition, agencies can now use simplified procedures for soliciting and evaluating bids up to $100,000. Government agencies, however, are still required to advertise all planned purchases over $25,000 in *www.FedBizOpps.gov*.

Simplified procedures require fewer administrative details, lower approval levels, and less documentation. New procurement reform legislation requires all federal purchases above $3,000 but under $100,000 to be reserved for small businesses, unless the contracting officer cannot obtain offers from two or more small businesses that are competitive on price, quality and delivery.

Government purchases of up to $3,000 in individual items or multiple items whose aggregate amount does not exceed $3,000 are now classified as "micro-purchases" and can be made without obtaining competitive quotes. However, these purchases are no longer reserved for small businesses.

Agencies can make micro-purchases using a Government Purchase Card (typical credit card).

Sealed Bidding

Sealed bidding is how the government contracts competitively when its requirements are clear, accurate and complete. An Invitation For Bid (IFB) is the method used for the sealed bid process. Typically, an IFB includes a description of the product or service to be acquired, instructions for preparing a bid, the conditions for purchase, packaging, delivery, shipping and payment, contract clauses to be included and the deadline for submitting bids. Each sealed bid is opened in public at the purchasing office at the time designated in the invitation. All bids are read aloud and recorded. A contract is then awarded by the agency to the low bidder who is determined to be responsive to the government's needs. Government-wide IFBs are available daily for review at FedBizOpps. This electronic government service also provides a direct link to the invitation.

Contracting officials search the **Central Contractor Registration** (CCR) to identify qualified small business contractors. Therefore, any small business that wants to sell to the government should be registered on CCR (*www.ccr.gov*).

Contract Negotiation

In certain cases, when the value of a government contract exceeds $100,000 and when it necessitates a highly technical product or service, the government may issue a Request for Proposal (RFP). In a typical RFP, the government will request a product or service it needs, and solicit proposals from prospective contractors on how they intend to carry out that request, and at what price. Proposals in response to an RFP can be subject to negotiation after they have been submitted.

When the government is merely checking into the possibility of acquiring a product or service, it may issue a Request for Quotation (RFQ). A response to an RFQ by a prospective contractor is not considered an offer, and consequently, cannot be accepted by the government to form a binding contract. The order is an offer by the government to the supplier to buy certain supplies or services upon specified terms and conditions. A contract is established when a supplier accepts the offer.

Government-wide RFPs and RFQs are available daily for review at FedBizOpps. This electronic government service also provides a direct link to the request. In most instances, the government uses oral solicitations for purchases less than $25,000, written solicitations for purchases over $25,000, and purchase cards to obtain micro-purchases less than $3.000.

One of the most significant changes government acquisition reforms is the increased importance of "best value." Best value means that, rather than making awards to the lowest bidder as it generally did in the past, the government can now make awards for the item that best satisfies its needs at a slightly higher price. If purchasers are going to make an award based on best value, they must state their intent in the solicitation document and include a description of the evaluation criteria, award factors, and factors other than the price that will be considered in making a contract award.

Consolidated Purchasing Programs

Most government agencies have common purchasing needs—carpeting, furniture, office machine maintenance, petroleum products and perishable food supplies are just a few examples. Sometimes the government can realize economies of scale by centralizing the purchasing of certain types of products or services.

Acquisition Vehicles - Procurement reform has ushered numerous new and/or modified acquisition vehicles--multiple award contracts--such as multi-agency contracts and government-wide acquisition contracts (**GWACs**). These vehicles encourage long-term vendor agreements with fewer vendors.

> **Governmentwide Acquisition Contracts (GWACs)** are defined in Part 2 of the Federal Acquisition Regulation (FAR) as task order or delivery order contracts for Information Technology (IT) established by one agency for government-wide use. Each GWAC is operated by an executive agent designated by the Office of Management and Budget (OMB) pursuant to section 5112(e) of the Clinger-Cohen Act. The Economy Act does not apply when placing orders under GWACs. To use GWACs, agencies must obtain a delegation of authority from the GWAC Program Office.

The use of these contract vehicles, including expanded use of GSA schedules has increased significantly during the last few years. These popular vehicles allow government buyers to quickly fill requirements by issuing orders against existing contracts or schedules without starting a new procurement action from scratch. Further, agencies can competitively award several or multiple task order contracts to different firms for the same products and services. This practice allows federal buyers to issue orders to any one or combination of several firms with relative ease.

The General Services Administration, the Defense Logistics Agency, and the Department of Veterans Affairs administer the three largest interagency consolidated purchasing programs.

Knowing what and how the government buys is essential if a business owner is to be successful in government contracting. Don't think, however, that you can relax once you receive the good news that you have won a contract. Your work is just beginning. If you cannot perform according to the terms of the contract, the government will not get the product or service it needs and you may find yourself in financial difficulty as well.

The first thing to do is to read the proposed contract carefully before signing it. This may look like an imposing task, as some contracts may contain many pages, depending on the type of contract and complexity of what the government is buying. However, many contract terms and conditions are "boiler plate." Once you read and understand the terms, you will be familiar with them when they appear in your next contract.

One important feature of the contract is the identity of the office that will administer it. In most federal agencies this is usually the same office that awarded the contract. In the Department of Defense, however, the contract is generally assigned to a special administering office. If you have any questions about the contract, contact the office of administration. Do not proceed and find out much later that you are not in compliance.

Specific Contract Administration Matters

While federal contracts are similar to commercial contracts, they are different in some very important ways. They contain or make reference to many general contract provisions unique to the government. These provisions implement various statutory or regulatory requirements applicable solely to federal contracts. Some of the important matters covered by these provisions are termination for default, termination for convenience, contract changes, payments, specifications, and inspection and testing. These matters are described in various parts of the Federal Acquisition Regulations.

Termination for Default

Government contracts provide that the government may cancel (terminate) your contract if:

- You fail to make delivery within the time specified in the contract;
- You fail to make progress so as to endanger performance of the contract; and/or
- You fail to perform any provisions of the contract.

Before terminating a contract for default, the contracting officer must give you an opportunity to remedy defects in your performance or show why your contract should not be terminated. If your contract is terminated for default, you are entitled only to payment at the contract's price for items accepted by the government. If the government still needs the items that you failed to deliver, it has the right to procure the same items elsewhere and, if they cost more, charge the excess costs to you. This can be a very serious and costly matter.

If you can show that your failure to deliver or to make progress is excusable, your contract will not be terminated for default. To be excusable, a delay must be beyond your control and not caused by your fault or negligence. If your contract is terminated for default and you can prove that the government's action was improper, the termination will be treated as one for the "convenience of the government."

Termination for Convenience

The government may unilaterally terminate all or part of a contract for its convenience. This type of termination does not arise from any fault on the part of the contractor. Termination for convenience protects the government's interests by allowing it to cancel contracts for products that become obsolete or unnecessary.

As with terminations for default, the government must give you written notice of termination for convenience, but is not required to give advance notice. The notice of termination will usually direct you to: stop work, terminate subcontracts, place no further orders, communicate similar instructions to subcontractors and suppliers, and prepare a termination settlement claim.

If you fail to follow these directions, you do so at your own risk and expense. You should also receive detailed instructions as to the protection and preservation of all property that is or may become government-owned. After termination for convenience, the government will make a settlement with you to compensate you fully and fairly for the work you have done and any preparation made for the terminated portion of the contract. A reasonable allowance for profit is also included.

Contract Changes

Because the government's needs change from time to time, government contracts contain a clause authorizing the contracting officer to unilaterally order changes in the specifications and other contract terms. The changes must be "within the general scope of the contract." The contractor is obliged to perform the contract as unilaterally changed by the contracting officer. A change is within the scope of the contract if it can be regarded as within the contemplation of the parties at the time the contract was entered into. The government cannot use a change order to change the general nature of the contract. The contractor is entitled to an equitable adjustment in price and delivery schedule if changes are ordered.

Payments

The obligation to make prompt payments for products delivered or services rendered is, generally speaking, the primary obligation of the government on a procurement contract. Payment is, naturally, of utmost importance to the small business. Your contract will specify the government office responsible for payment and will contain invoicing instructions. The more accurate your invoices, the more quickly you will be paid, so it is important to understand the payment process thoroughly. Prompt payment on all contracts serves the best interest of both the contractor and the government. Under certain circumstances if the government does not accomplish prompt payment, you can submit a request for interest payments. (*Reference: Public Law 97-177, Prompt Payment Act.*)

Under fixed-price contracts, the method of payment can vary with the dollar value of the contract. For relatively small contracts with a single item of work, you will generally be paid the total contract price in one lump sum. Payment is made after the government accepts delivery. For larger contracts with many items, you can invoice and receive partial payments. For example, in a contract for 120 units with a delivery rate of 10 per month, you can invoice each month for the price of delivered (and accepted) items.

Larger fixed-price contracts and subcontracts where the first delivery is several months after award may contain a clause permitting you to receive progress payments based upon costs incurred as work progresses.

Because progress payments are based on work that is not completed, you must repay them if you fail to complete the work. To protect its interest, the government takes title to your work-in-process for which progress payments have been made. To qualify for progress payments, you must have an accounting system that can accurately identify and segregate contract costs.

Specifications

The federal government has exact specifications for most of the products and services it buys on a regular basis. In all likelihood, your contract will contain such precise specifications. Specifications that describe the government's requirements were contained in the invitation for bids or request for proposals on which you based your bid or proposal.

Once an award is made to your company, you are contractually bound to deliver the product or service described in the specifications. Sometimes, the basic specifications will make reference to and incorporate other federal specifications. You are, of course, bound by the terms of these specifications as well as the basic specifications. Failure to deliver a product meeting these terms may result in termination of your contract by default.

Accordingly, never bid on a contract unless you have read and understood all of the specifications. Also, read the specifications again before you start work under the contract.

Inspection and Testing

Government contracts provide that the government may inspect and test the items you deliver to determine if they conform to contract requirements and specifications. The government will not accept a contractor's product unless it passes inspection. The type and extent of inspection and testing depend largely on what is being procured.

Special Recommendations and Advice

In addition to knowing the item you are manufacturing or the service you are providing, you should have a working knowledge of government contracting procedures, some of which are explained in this publication. You should also be aware of the following:

- The government conducts its business through authorized agents called contracting officers. Only a contracting officer has authority to bind the government, unless you are otherwise advised in writing. However, even contracting officers have limits on their authority. Don't hesitate to make sure of the authority of the person with whom you are dealing.

- Government procurement has historically been used as a vehicle for advancing various national, social and economic objectives. As a government contractor, you will be required to comply with the labor standards statutes (Service Contract Act, Contract Work Hours and Safety Standards Act, etc.) and other statutes advancing national socio-economic objectives, except for certain contracts where such legislation is specifically stated as non-applicable.

- You should become familiar with the contract provisions protecting the integrity of the government procurement process. These provisions include the "officials not to benefit" clause, the "anti-kickback" provisions, the "gratuities" clause, etc.

- Disputes between you and the contracting officer may occur under the contract. Federal contracts contain a clause setting forth procedures to resolve disputes. If the contracting officer issues a decision that is not satisfactory to you, you must make a timely appeal or the decision becomes final. Appeals are heard by the Board of Contracts Appeal.

- Do not attempt to build something bigger, better or different than called for by the contract. If you do, it may be too big or too heavy or may not fit and the government will not accept it. Simply comply with the contract terms, particularly the specifications.

- If your contract requires production, establish a production control schedule to assure that you will have the right materials in-house at the right time to meet delivery requirements. Make sure to place any subcontracts promptly and schedule delivery of subcontracted items carefully to avoid over-or-under stocking. If it appears you will not meet your schedule, notify the administration office immediately to obtain assistance. Failure to deliver on time gives the government the right to cancel your contract, with possibly disastrous results to you.

- One of the first things that must be done by a small business is to market to the Federal government. The best ways to start include registering on SBA's PRO-Net database, and contracting the agency's office of small and disadvantaged business utilization (OSDBU).

- Being e-commerce savvy is very important in doing business with the federal government. For example, if you want to do business with the Department of Defense, you must be able to invoice and receive payments electronically. Therefore, small business owners interested in doing business with the federal government should master electronic commerce.

Identifying Your Business

Clearly defining your business is important for accurate representation of your firm when submitting contract proposals. In addition, such identification can serve as a marketing strategy.

Are You a Small Business?

Small business size standards are based on the North American Industry Classification System (NAICS), a six-digit system that replaced SIC codes.

The new NAICS system was developed to reorganize business categories on a production/process-oriented basis. The purpose behind the creation of the NAICS classification system is specifically for governmental regulations and census reports.

Federal Supply Classification (FSC) - identifies products

The federal government uses numeric federal supply class (FSC) codes to describe the supplies, products and commodities it purchases. Learn how to classify products. Visit SBA's website for further information.

Subcontracting Opportunities

Subcontracting or teaming with a prime contractor can be a profitable experience as well as a growth opportunity for your business. If, after assessing the capabilities and capacity of your business, you conclude that you are not ready to bid competitively for prime contracts, consider the opportunities available through subcontracting. The experience gained from performing as a subcontractor can assist you in responding to solicitations as a prime contractor. Subcontracting, however, should not be viewed only as an opportunity for less-experienced business, but also as a vehicle to enhance your qualifications to become more competitive to perform as a prime contractor.

Over the years, several laws have been passed regarding subcontracting to small business. All of these are now incorporated into Section 8(d) of the Small Business Act and, in most cases, FAR 19.7. These laws require prime contractors having contracts that exceed the simplified acquisition threshold (SAT) to provide maximum practicable subcontracting opportunities to small business, HUBZone small business, small disadvantaged business, women-owned small business, veteran-owned small business (VOSB), and service-disabled VOSB. The clause "Utilization of Small Business Concerns," must be included in all federal contracts exceeding the SAT.

These laws, among other things, require that:

- On contracts more than $500,000 (or $1,000,000 for construction of a public facility) large prime contractors and other-than-small subcontractors submit subcontracting plans containing specific percentage goals for small business, HUBZone small business, small disadvantaged business, women-owned small business, VOSB, and service-disabled VOSB.

- Subcontracting plans must contain a description of the methods and efforts used to assure that small business enterprises have an equitable opportunity to compete for subcontracts.

- Subcontracting plans must be submitted by contractors for review prior to the award of any contract, failure to comply in good faith with its approved plan may subject the contractor to liquidated damages or termination for default.

The requirement to submit a subcontracting plan does not apply to:

- Small businesses,
- Contracts under the prescribed dollar amounts,
- Prime contracts not offering subcontracting possibilities, or
- Contracts to be performed entirely outside the United States

SBA's Recommendations

As a small business engaged in subcontracting, be sure you understand the terms and conditions of your contract with the prime contractor before agreeing to serve as a subcontractor. Ask:

- How and when will I receive compensation from the prime contractor?

- How much can I rely on the prime contractor for special tools, engineering advice, information on manufacturing methods, etc.?

- How will quality control and inspection procedures be applied to my subcontract?

Find subcontracting opportunities at SBA SUB-Net (*http://web.sba.gov/subnet*).

Building on the foregoing introduction, Chapter One, which follows, imparts OSDBU *Gems of Wisdom*.

OSDBUs
Impart
Gems of Wisdom

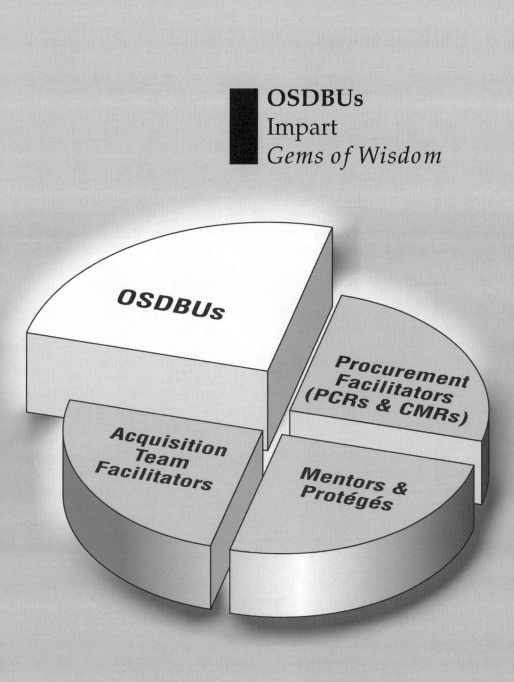

OSDBUs Impart *Gems of Wisdom*

OSDBUs are an integral part of the extended business development network for 8(a)BD firms. When they perform optimally and work hand-in-glove with Procurement Center Representatives (PCRs), a perfect storm of business development assistance can be rendered to help 8(a)BD firms increase their competitiveness.

The law is clear: Each federal agency is meant to have an Office of Small and Disadvantaged Business Utilization (OSDBU) that plays an advocacy role by overseeing the agency's functions and duties related to the awarding of contracts and subcontracts to small and disadvantaged businesses. To advocate effectively for small and disadvantaged businesses, the Small Business Act requires that the OSDBU directors be responsible to and report only to agency heads (or their deputies) so that the directors have immediate access to their agency's top decision-makers.

That's the law. The reality can be different. It's also the law that all OSDBUs were created equal, but they don't necessarily perform equally.

Therefore, it's wise to heed the advice of Ralph Thomas, former NASA OSDBU Director, who says: "The first thing 8(a)BD firms should ascertain is how each OSDBU office works in practice. Understand what functions the OSDBUs of different agencies perform and what their staff are willing to do for firms."

A few years ago, when Thomas was involved with the OSDBU Interagency Council, a document was prepared, a *"Model Code of Expectations,"* which set forth guidelines for what the OSDBUs should do for clients and what clients should do when requesting assistance from them. It's useful to be reminded of these "common sense" expectations, which are shown in Box 1.

Box 1

**Model Code of Expectations
Between
Federal Offices of Small and Disadvantaged Business Utilization
(OSDBUs)
And
Small Businesses**

**Developed by the External Liaison Committee of the
Federal OSDBU Directors Interagency Council
(August 2003)**

Small Businesses can expect that the OSDBU will:

• Make very clear up front the depth and breadth of the services that can be expected from the OSDBU;

• Be exceptionally candid as to whether the capabilities of the small business match the agency's needs, and, if not, direct them to the appropriate OSDBU or prime contractor Small Business Liaison Officer (SBLO), preferably with a personal introduction;

• Explain the relevant laws enacted for their benefit, i.e., small business set-asides, 8(a) set-asides, HUBZone set-asides, subcontracting goals, and illustrate how the small business can use them to maximize contract and subcontract opportunities;

• Put them in contact with the appropriate project/technical managers, end users, or any other relevant personnel, assuming the small business is selling what the OSDBU's agency is buying;

• Inform small businesses with all up- to- date information in light of the ever-changing procurement legislation and implementing regulations that impact small business;

• Be a "marketing consultant," "information broker," and facilitator to the small business, e.g., inform it of any special unwritten and cultural nuances or procedures at the OSDBU's agency and its buying activities that will improve the small business' chances of winning a contract;

• Make very clear that certification as an 8(a), small disadvantaged business, HUBZone contractor, service disabled veteran does not create an *entitlement* to a contract or a guarantee for one in the future;

• Stress that understanding the agency's procurement process, engaging in strong marketing, and competing for work, even sole source work, is critical to enhancing one's prospects of obtaining a contract;

• Ensure a professionally conducted meeting with time parameters and expectations set in advance;

• Summarize the agency's contracting opportunities at its various contracting activities and field installations for the small business' specific area of business or make referrals to those places where the small business can go to obtain such knowledge;

• Demonstrate, if necessary, how to navigate within the agency's host website and highlight the most useful sites and links;

• Offer follow-up due date for responding to questions for which the OSDBU counselor does not have an immediate answer;

• Impart knowledge about the "market" (what the OSDBU's agency buys), the decision makers (agency key players) and the competitive environment at the agency (who the incumbents are, what service needs are growing, which are declining, where the future strategic, long term opportunities are, etc.);

• Not give false hope, vague or generic information, such as stating how many millions or billions of dollars the agency spends on goods and services with no explanation as to how the small business can reasonably expect to fit into the agency's procurement structure or system;

• Treat all small businesses the same under like circumstances when providing pertinent procurement information and not show special preference to a network of friends or acquaintances;

• Provide information on the agency's latest acquisition-related initiatives and agency unique programs that will, or were designed to, increase the chances of a small business to obtain a contract or subcontract, e.g. discuss agency's mentor-protégé program, if applicable.

The OSDBU can expect that the small business will:

• Have done preliminary research on the agency's website and other sources of information to determine what their mission is and whether it buys what the small business sells;

• Be focused on discussing its area of expertise based on requirements;

• Be cognizant of time and schedule and does not prolong the discussion past the time set for the meeting;

• Make a case as to why an agency should use its firm over other small businesses that perform the same type of work or provide the same products;

• Not develop unrealistic expectations based upon the meeting;

• Be aware that the OSDBU is not the end user and does not need to hear the entire technical marketing presentation;

• Follow the recommended avenues of opportunity outlined by the OSDBU that the firm determines are consistent with its best interests;

• Understand that various small business certifications, i.e., 8(a), SDB, HUBZone, women owned small businesses, service disabled veterans, are secondary to a small business' ability to emphasize its high quality products or services, on time delivery, and best value;

• Understand that from an ethical and legal standpoint that an OSDBU CANNOT:
– Promise anyone a contract;
– Provide government-proprietary information;

- Share third party proprietary information;
- Direct large contractors to provide jobs (employment or subcontracting) to a particular small business;
- Help small businesses write/review proposals to be submitted to the OSDBU's agency or any other government agency;
- Act in a manner that is tantamount to acting as an agent of the small business.

The wisdom of this advice holds up over time and should be heeded. Thomas provides further time-tested and value-added advice that 8(a)BD firms should bear in mind when seeking assistance to break into federal government procurements. According to Thomas, there are four essential questions that 8(a)BD firms must understand about the agencies with which they are seeking to do business:

■ Does the agency buy what I sell?
■ How does the agency purchase it?
■ When does the agency purchase it?
■ Who in the agency purchases it?

During his 17 years at NASA's OSDBU, Thomas has heard it all from 8(a)BD firms and other small businesses. He knows firsthand what works and what doesn't when firms try to pitch to the OSDBUs and to other agency officials.

What doesn't work, he underscores, is for firms to focus—*in the few minutes they are allotted for a face-to-face meeting*—on their corporate qualifications rather than on past performance.

The key to making a positive impression is to highlight what the firm has done and how it is relevant to what the agency is currently seeking. Two things are implicit: First, the firm should have past performance experience, and secondly, the experience should be relevant to what the agency is buying today.

Thomas advises, "Have a 25 second speech ready when you get a meeting with either OSDBU staff or other agency officials. Ensure that in addition to focusing on past performance that the performance cited highlights the successes you have had. Establish your 'competitive discriminators' right away, and present examples of them."

If the first contact goes well, according to Thomas, and you may get a second follow up meeting. In the second meeting, provide additional information about past performance successes. "Be brief and succinct, keep it relevant, and don't overwhelm the audience," advises Thomas. "The first and second meetings are only the starting place; the whole process takes time. Firms must be patient and realize that they must stay in front of their marketing targets," Thomas adds. The most critical thing is for firms to provide relevant examples of their accomplishments whenever they do make contact.

The Minority Business Guide - 2004-2005 Premier Edition THE MINORITY BUSINESS

Ralph C. Thomas, III
Assistant Administrator for Small and Disadvantaged Business Utilization
National Aeronautics and Space Administration (NASA)
www.osdbu.nasa.gov

Expert Editorial

Four Essential Questions for Successful Marketing to the Federal Government

The other day I received an interesting email from a small business owner. He had just gotten my notice about an upcoming procurement conference. His reply didn't pull any punches. "I'm tired of going to all of these conferences, seminars, and workshops," he wrote. "Those things are just a waste of my time. What I want is a contract." I'm sure that sentiment echoes the feelings of a lot of small business that want to do business with the Federal government. However, his response is clear evidence that he was missing valuable opportunities for scoring Federal contracts by the way he viewed small business conferences.

First of all, as a small business, your goal in attending a procurement conference should not be to obtain a contract. That is not to say that it does not happen on occasion. It does. However, you should consider that a windfall. Primarily, you should go to a conference to gather enough information to determine what the best contract opportunities are on which to focus your limited resources. You must go after the contract that affords you the best possible chance of winning. You can do this by asking four essential questions of the individual standing behind an exhibit table or booth.

The first question you should ask the government agency representative is, "do you buy what my company sells?" The answer to this question is central to whether or not you invest any more of your time asking follow-up questions. Do not be disappointed if the answer is "no." You merely move on to the next table. There is no sense spending time talking to someone who does not want or need what you sell.

If the answer to the first question is "yes," however, the second question is, "how do you buy what I sell?" This is extremely important, too. For example, do they buy it through the 8(a) program,

You must go after the contract that affords you the best possible chance of winning. You can do this by asking four essential questions of the individual standing behind an exhibit table or booth.

or do they get it from a large business as a result of a full and open competition? Does the agency buy it off the GSA Schedule or off of a Government-wide Acquisition Contract (GWAC)? Is it bought from a company as a result of a small business set-aside competition? The answer to this question will also be pertinent to whether or not you decide to pursue marketing this particular agency.

The third question is, "who buys the product or service that you sell?" Remember that in most cases the small business specialist for any Federal agency is merely your starting point in your marketing for a contract. Your goal is to get to the "end user" - the individual who actually purchases what you sell. It is important to remember not to market to a Government Small Business Program Advisor the same way you would market to the end user. The Small Business Advisor does not buy anything unless, of course, it is the end user. Usually, however, that is not the case. Save the elaborate details of what you can do and how well you can do it for the end user - someone who will generally understand what you are talking about.

Finally, you want to ask when the agency buys what you sell. This is very important for marketing purposes. For example, if the agency buys the services under the 8(a) program, and you are an 8(a) contractor, you want to know when the current contract ends. The longer away from the termination date it is, the longer you will have to plan and implement your marketing strategy. If the contract is expiring within the year, however, it might be too late.

Asking the four essential questions will not necessarily guarantee you a Federal contract. However, it will allow you to save more of your valuable time and money, thereby enabling you to focus your marketing on those contract opportunities that provide you the best possible chance of winning.

What 8(a)BD firms must realize, Thomas further underscores, is that agency officials, prime contractors, OSDBU officials and other marketing targets are inundated by requests to meet small businesses. Therefore, it's incumbent upon 8(a)BD firms to focus on their "competitive discriminators." Certifications, regardless of what they are, are not competitive discriminators. Successfully executed and relevant past performance is what it's all about. Thomas has been preaching this for some time, as his article in the *Minority Business Guide's* 2004-2005 Edition attests.

Verl Zanders, who served in various compacities in the government, including as Director of Small Business Programs at the Office of the Secretary, U.S. Department of Health and Human Services (HHS) for over 10 years, is an entrepreneur today. He knows the drill. He adds a fifth essential question to those identified by Ralph Thomas. He advises:

> "In addition to posing four essential questions about agency procurements, pose a fifth: *Who is the agency buying it from*?"

A long journey of research is ahead to answer the question, according to Zanders. "What an 8(a)BD firm should be looking for in the success of others is a model," Zanders underscores. He adds: "A model is not a mentor." Rather, a model is a firm that is in a similar line of business but which has the benefit of more experience and success under its belt. A model is the firm you seek to become like; it's an aspirational goal.

> "It's only when you know where you want to go that you can chart a path for getting there."

"No matter what path you may seek to chart, other firms have already charted it." As Zanders puts it, "The game is old, the only thing new if your firm." The trick, he says, is to identify which firm you'd like to model your firm on and follow that leader.

"In searching for role models, don't stop at one agency in looking at the contracts 'your model firm' has; examine the contracts they have in different agencies as well. This research will tell you a lot," Zanders says.

Formulating strategic goals enables firms to better utilize the assistance of the OSDBUs, and heeding the advice rendered in the first four points of the "Code of Expectations" for small businesses is the key to having productive interchanges with the OSDBU.

One of the first steps in getting to know the OSDBU is to study its website and that of the agency of which it's a part.

The importance of utilizing the websites of the OSDBUs can't be overstated. They contain valuable resources for helping 8(a)BDs market to respective agencies.

At the same time, 8(a)BD firms are reminded that while they are searching the agency's websites, agency officials may also be searching their website as well. Therefore, it's important for firms to keep their websites updated and to highlight positive past performance on them.

Regarding OSDBU websites, while all of the information presented is useful particular attention is drawn to the agency's **procurement forecast**, **mentor-protégé programs**, if applicable, and lists of **prime contractors** that are interested in working with subcontractors.

Take the Department of Homeland Security (DHS), as one example. Its total small business goal, as of FY 2007, was 30 percent, out of which the goal for 8(a)BD firms was 4 percent. To make their goals, DHS alerts small businesses to agency forecasts and provides information about prime contractors and participants in its Mentor-Protégé program. The latter information is useful to help 8(a)BD identify larger firms that may wish to approach for future relationships.

The following information, presented by DHS, but which is representative of that typically provided by OSDBUs on its websites, is shown below. Such websites are marketing resources that 8(a)BDs should take advantage of when marketing to agencies. Information presented includes: (*http://www.dhs.gov/xopnbiz/smallbusiness/index.shtm*:

Small Business Points of Contact:
- *Small Business Specialists* - Points of contact for Department of Homeland Security's eight buying activities;

- *OSDBU Staff* - overall information on the Department of Homeland Security Small Business program;

- *Frequently Asked Questions* (FAQs);

- *Forecast of Contract Opportunities* - Projections of all anticipated contract actions above $100,000;

- *Prime Contractors* - Information on subcontracting opportunities with Homeland Security large business Prime Contractors.

Outreach

- *Vendor Outreach Sessions* (VOS) for FY 2008 - Pre-arranged 15-minute appointments with representatives from Homeland Security Organizational Elements;

- *Small Business Conferences* attended by Homeland Security, Office of Small and Disadvantaged Business Utilization (OSDBU) personnel;

- *Mentor-Protégé Program* - Program designed to foster mentoring relationships between Homeland Security prime contractors and small businesses;

- *Mentor-Protégé Companies.* Points of contact are given for each mentor and protégé in the program; (*http://www.dhs.gov/xopnbiz/smallbusiness/gc_1198248049694.shtm*)

- *8(a)BD Competitive Current Opportunities.* Points of contact are given for pre-solicitation notices.

In addition to the foregoing, DHS provides useful information about contracting opportunities (*http://www.dhs.gov/xopnbiz/opportunities/index.shtm*), such as lists of:

- Homeland Security Contracting Opportunities through FedBizOpps;

- Information Technology Acquisitions (EAGLE, FirstSource);

- Hurricane Katrina Emergency Contracting Opportunities.

Selected forecasts of contract opportunities are also provided, which include for instance:

- DHS Advance Acquisition Planning: Forecast of Contract Opportunities, which includes projections of all anticipated contract actions greater than $100,000;

- EAGLE IT Procurement Forecast;

- Homeland Security Advanced Research Projects Agency (HSARPA);

- HSARPA Small Business Innovation Research (SBIR) Program;

- Domestic Nuclear Detection Office (DNDO) Business Opportunities;

- SAFECOM Program

Small Business Prime Contracting Accomplishments Fiscal Year 2006		
Category	Goal (%)	Accomplishment ($ and %)
Total Procurement Dollars	N/A	$13,918,214,299
SB Prime Contracts	30.0%	$4,400,575,711 / 31.62%
SDB Prime Contracts [overall; including 8(a) contracts]	8.0%	$1,496,530,345 / 10.75%
8(a) Contracts	4.0%	$860,671,324 / 6.18%
SDB Prime Contracts [other than 8(a)]	4.0%	$635,859,021 / 4.57%
HUBZone SB Prime Contracts	3.0%	$460,250,699 / 3.31%
SDVOSB Prime Contracts	3.0%	$214,054,627 / 1.54%
WOSB Prime Contracts	5.0%	$933,469,517 / 6.71%

DHS is taken as just one example; all OSDBUs have websites and all of their websites are useful for marketing purposes.

Take the U.S. Department of Energy, the largest civilian buying agency, as another example. Its OSDBU's goal is to help small firms get a piece of the over $22 billion in goods and services procured by the agency each year. Its website *(http://smallbusiness.doe.gov)* provides a comprehensive guide for *Doing Business With DOE*, information about its monthly business opportunity sessions, information about its annual conferences, and most importantly, it presents information on DOE's Acquisition Forecast of Prime Contracting and Subcontracting Opportunities.

DOE's Office of Minority Economic Impact Director, Theresa Speake, is a strong supporter of the 8(a)BD program. Under her leadership an innovative 8(a)BD program has been piloted.

> **The DOE 8(a)BD Pilot Program**: As a leader in providing contracting and subcontracting opportunities to small businesses, the Department of Energy (DOE) continues to challenge the private sector by encouraging its major prime contractors to seek ways to include small businesses in its procurement process. A very effective vehicle used in developing subcontracting opportunities for small disadvantaged businesses was the introduction into the procurement process of the "8(a)BD Pilot Program." The "8(a)BD Pilot Program," hereafter referred to as "the

Program," was established in FY 1991 to: 1) target 8(a)BD businesses for DOE procurement opportunities at the subcontract level; 2) to allow flexibility to DOE's major prime contractors in awarding subcontracts to 8(a)BD business concerns; and 3) to create additional ways for 8(a)BD businesses to access the economic mainstream of American society. The Program, which is voluntary to DOE's major prime contractors, achieved $167,182 in its first year of operation. The Program's achievement has grown to more than $150 million today.

The Program strengthens DOE's support of the federal 8(a)BD Program administered by the U.S. Small Business Administration (SBA). The Small Business Act (15 U.S.C. 644) authorizes the SBA to enter into contracts for goods and services with other federal agencies, and reserve up to a value of $3.5 million ($5.5 million for manufacturing) in contracts non-competitively to 8(a)BD certified firms. If a procurement is valued in excess of $3.5 million ($5.5 million for manufacturing) and two or more capable 8(a)BD firms can be so identified, the procurement shall be set-aside for competition among 8(a)BD firms (see FAR 19.805-1(a) (2)).

Benefits of the Program

The Program is popular among 8(a)BD certified firms as it mimics the SBA 8(a)BD Program and has similar benefits for its participants, e.g.:

- Participants can receive sole-source contracts up to $3.5 million for goods and services, and $5.5 million for manufacturing.

- Participants can bid/propose on competitive procurements above $3.5 million for goods and services, and above $5.5 million for manufacturing that are set-aside for 8(a)BD participation only.

- Participants gain a prime position to market private sector firms to become a protégé.

- Participants gain a prime position to partner with its private sector prime contractor in order to obtain future procurement opportunities.

Program Operations

Small business contractors that are 8(a)BD certified and interested in seeking 8(a)BD business opportunities with

DOE's major prime contractors should access the *"Directory of Small Business Managers"* to identify prime contractors that participate in the Program. A listing of major prime contractors participating in the Program is available by contacting the OSDBU. When an 8(a)BD firm receives a contract from a DOE prime contractor participating in the Program, the contract becomes a bilateral agreement between the prime contractor and the 8(a)BD business concern. Prime contractors that wish to identify 8(a)BD business concerns to perform its work may use its own sources or contact the OSDBU.

Speake appreciates that the 8(a)BD program is a business development program. From her perspective at Energy, where the contract sizes are very large, one of the best ways to meet the business development objectives of the 8(a)BD program is participation in the Mentor-Protégé program. Mentoring, according to Speake, "helps a business develop in very practical and measurable ways."

> **Purpose of the Mentor-Protégé Program:** The Office of Small and Disadvantaged Business Utilization continually strives to increase subcontracting opportunities by encouraging prime contractors to assist small disadvantaged businesses through participation in the Department's Mentor Protégé Program. Those eligible for the Program include:
>
> - 8(a)BD businesses and other small disadvantaged businesses
> - Women-owned businesses
> - Service disabled veteran-owned businesses
> - HUBZone Businesses
> - Historically Black College and University (HBCUs) and other Minority Educational Institutions
>
> The Department of Energy's Facility Management Contractors which have been approved as mentors firms may enter into agreements with eligible small disadvantaged businesses as protégé firms to provide appropriate developmental assistance to enhance the business and technical capabilities of small disadvantaged businesses to perform as contractors, subcontractors, and suppliers.

The working arrangement between companies will promote economic and technological growth, promote and foster the establishment of long term business relationships and increase the number of small disadvantaged businesses which receive Department of Energy, and other federal agency and commercial contract.

Mentor-Protégé Program Requirements

Mentors: A prime contractor performing at least one active DOE Contract.

Protégés:

- Must be a small business certified as an 8 (a) business, other small disadvantaged, a women-owned small business, service disabled veteran-owned small business, HUBZone small business, HBCU, or minority educational Institution

- Must be eligible to receive government contracts

- Must have been in business for a period not less than 2 years prior to application

- Must be able to certify as a small business according to the North American Industrial Code for the services or supplies to be provided by the Protégé under the subcontract with the Mentor.

Examples of Developmental Assistance Provided By Mentors:

a. Management guidance relating to:
    Financial management
    Organizational management
    Overall business management planning
    Business development, and marketing assistance

b. Engineering and other technical assistance;

c. Noncompetitive award of subcontracts under DOE or other federal contracts where otherwise authorized;

d. Award of subcontracts in the mentor's commercial activities;

e. Progress payments based on costs;

f. Rent-free use of facilities and/or equipment owned or leased by mentor;

g. Temporary assignment of mentor personnel to the Protégé for purposes of training.

"The Mentor-Protégé program is a win-win for everybody," Speake explains. The Mentor wins by being able to get involved in contracts set aside for small business; the Protégé wins by learning critical business develop tools such as scheduling, proposal writing, and project management, among other skills; and agencies win by being able to meet their 8(a)BD goals through getting 8(a)BD firms involved in larger contracts than might have otherwise been the case.

The Protégé is not the only one that learns in the Mentor-Protégé relationship, however. Mentors also learn from Protégés. For instance, the Protégé might be stronger in a given market than a Mentor, in which case the Mentor can learn from the Protégé.

Speake advises 8(a)BD firms to get involved in a Mentor-Protégé relationship. A starting place in the exploration, she advises, is for 8(a)BD firms to get a list of Mentors and Protégés in the different federal government programs and to research their agreements. Where possible, they should also ascertain from them what worked and what didn't work in the relationship.

The importance of doing one's homework in advance of entering into a mentor-protégé relationship can't be over-emphasized. A perfect example was given in a September 2007 issue of Washington Technology:

> Innovative Management and Technology Services LLC, based in Fairmont, W.Va., inherited a mentor-protégé relationship with Lockheed Martin Corp. when IMTS acquired DN American Inc. in 2005.
>
> Chirag Patel, president and chief executive officer of IMTS, said the relationship has been helpful to his company.
>
> IMTS, which will graduate from the 8(a)BD program in 2010, already had some federal business, including a contract with the FBI Criminal Justice Information Center in Clarksburg, W.Va. Also, DN American brought a relationship with a NASA facility in Fairmont. But in the years since the acquisition, IMTS has won work with

agencies in Washington and Cleveland after the Mentor-Protégé program opened doors.

But the transition wasn't seamless. If Patel could start fresh, he said, he'd choose a group in Lockheed Martin more directly attuned to the company's plans. The companies had to make some adjustments to connect IMTS to the right parts of Lockheed Martin to square with the protégé's growth plans.

"We got into the mentor-protégé program not knowing we were going to get this far this fast," he said. "Post acquisition of DN American, we're now more focused on advanced IT services. We're fine-tuning our core competencies and our skill areas to where we want to be."

Reportedly, the U.S. Small Business Administration (SBA) is in the process of updating its database of current mentors and protégés. Once the information is available, it will undoubtedly be a useful resource for 8(a)BD firms that want to contact both mentors and protégés to learn about the usefulness of such relationships. At present, according to information reported in *Washington Technology*, September 2007:

The Small Business Administration has approved about 52 mentor/protégé relationships under its program this year [2007], and there are more than 150 active ones under SBA alone, said Joe Loddo, SBA's Director of the 8(a)BD business development program. Other agencies' programs are separate from SBA's.

Exactly how many federal agencies have Mentor-Protégé programs is not clear, some include, however, the Department of Defense, Energy, State, U.S. Agency for International Development, NASA, the Air Force, Homeland Security, and Transportation. The Department of Defense's program, launched in 1991 makes it easy for 8(a)BDs to undertake research on its programs. Its dedicated website (*http://www.acq.osd.mil/osbp/mentor_protege/*) lists all agreements, agreements by service, and all protégés and mentors. Similarly, a number of the other federal government agencies, such as DOE, DHS that have Mentor-Protégé programs also list their participants on the OSDBU websites.

Even after doing one's homework, Speake acknowledges that formulating an optimum mutually beneficial Mentor-Protégé agreement is easier said than done. The key consideration is for the 8(a)BD to understand what mentoring they need precisely, Speake advises. The agreement must ensure that the protégé receives the mentoring it needs, while also ensuring that, in accordance with regulatory requirements, the protégé is involved in a "significant" portion of the work under contract.

It's important to know the rules of the game, and the rules are:

§ 124.510 What percentage of work must a Participant perform on an 8(a)BD contract?

(a) To assist the business development of Participants in the 8(a)BD program, an 8(a)BD contractor must perform certain percentages of work with its own employees. These percentages and the requirements relating to them are the same as those established for small business set-aside prime contractors, and are set forth in §125.6 of this title.

(b) A Participant must certify in its offer that it will meet the applicable percentage of work requirement. SBA will determine whether the firm will be in compliance as of the date of award of the contract for both sealed bid and negotiated procurements.

(c) *Indefinite quantity contracts.* (1) In order to ensure that the required percentage of costs on an indefinite quantity 8(a)BD award is performed by the Participant, the Participant must demonstrate semiannually that it has performed the required percentage to that date. For a service or supply contract, this does not mean that the Participant must perform 50 percent of the applicable costs for each task order with its own force, or that a Participant must have performed 50 percent of the applicable costs at any point in time during the contract's life. Rather, the Participant must perform 50 percent of the applicable costs for the combined total of all task orders issued to date at six-month intervals.

> *Example to paragraph (c)(1).* Two task orders are issued under an 8(a)BD indefinite quantity service contract during the first six months of the contract. If $100,000 in personnel costs are incurred on the first task order, 90% of those costs ($90,000) are incurred for performance by the Participant's own work force, and the second task order also requires $100,000 in personnel costs, the Participant would have to perform only 10 percent of the personnel costs on the second task order because it would still have performed 50% of the total personnel costs at the end of the six-month period ($100,000 out of $200,000).

(2) Where there is a guaranteed minimum condition in an indefinite quantity 8(a)BD award, the required performance of work percentage need not be met on task orders issued during the first six months of the contract. In such a case, however, the percentage of work that a Participant may further contract to other concerns during the first six months of the contract may not exceed 50 percent of the total guaranteed minimum dollar value to be provided by the contract. Once the guaranteed minimum amount is met, the general rule for indefinite quantity contracts set forth in paragraph (c)(1) of this section applies.

> *Example to paragraph (c)(2).* Where a contract guarantees a minimum of $100,000 in professional services and the first task order is for $60,000 in such services, the Participant may perform as little as $10,000 of the personnel costs for that order. In such a case, however, the Participant must perform all of the next task order(s) up to $40,000 to ensure that it performs 50% of the $100,000 guaranteed minimum ($10,000 + $40,000 = $50,000 or 50% of the $100,000).

(3) The applicable SBA District Director may waive the provisions in paragraphs (c)(1) and (c)(2) of this section requiring a Participant to meet the applicable performance of work requirement at the end of any six-month period where he or she makes a written determination that larger amounts of subcontracting are essential during certain stages of performance, provided that there are written assurances from both the Participant and the procuring activity that the contract will ultimately comply with the requirements of this section. Where SBA authorizes a Participant to exceed the subcontracting limitations and the Participant does not ultimately comply with the performance of work requirements by the end of the contract, SBA will not grant future waivers for the Participant.

To meet its 8(a)BD goals, the DOE OSDBU facilitates the development of Mentor-Protégé agreements to "have them on the shelf ready to be activated" when the right procurement opportunity comes along. Toward this end, the OSDBU seeks list of protégés from SBA that it can match with mentors. The OSDBU also provides assistance in developing the agreements. Mentor-Protégé agreements are vitally important, according to Speake, and are the best hope for meeting 8(a)BD goals given the large value of DOE contracts.

8(a)BD firms are still very much in the game at Energy. As of FY 2007, the percentage of the overall small business goals of the agency represented by 8(a)BD goals was second only to that of SDB goals, as follows:

Small Business	8(a)BD	SDB	Women	HUBZone	Service Disabled Veteran
4.42%	1.22%	1.69%	0.39%	0.11%	0.08%

In dollars and sense, the total small business goals represent over $10 billion. It's critical, according to Speake, for 8(a)BD firms to enter into Mentor-Protégé agreements in order to develop their business and to get a larger share of Energy's procurement dollars.

LaVerne Drummond, who worked for the U.S. Agency for International Development in various capacities in the OSDBU office for almost two decades before retiring recently, agrees that the key to success for 8(a)BD firms is to build relationships. Whether such relationships are formalized in Mentor-Protégé agreements or not, it's nevertheless important to build a series of contacts and relationships with other firms and throughout government agencies. She advises firms to pay attention to outreach and network events OSDBUs sponsor, which are listed on the websites of the OSDBUs; they are valuable for providing a venue to meet other firms and contacts within agencies.

Given the scope of procurements within each federal agency, Drummond underscores the need to target certain types of activities that 8(a)BD firm might want to go after. This will enable the firm to focus its marketing activities on the right government officials and on the right potential partner firms. She also suggests that once a firm is clear about the kind of work they are looking for within an agency, they should be persistent or "friendly pushy" in establishing and maintaining contacts.

Importantly, in requesting assistance from the OSDBUs, 8(a)BD firms are reminded that the burden of responsibility on the OSDBUs to be helpful goes beyond merely providing information. They are meant to be advocates for small business and should be held accountable. In that regard, it's important to understand how OSDBUs do their work.

In approaching OSDBUs for assistance, according to Drummond, 8(a)BD firm owners must ask the right questions. For instance, discern whether the OSDBU is aggressive in identifying procurements for 8(a)BD firms. Question how they work with SBA liaison officers such as PCRs. Determine whether their forecasts have the required information for points of contacts to inquire about the opportunities. Determine if OSDBU staff can they easily steer you in the right direction to get information about previous contracts and contractors with the agency. Ask if they provide you with a copy of agency Management Reports, which discuss agency deficiencies.

Agency Management Reports and other strategic documents, such as Congressional Presentations are key in imparting a complete understanding of where the agency is going and where it's coming from. In other words, according to Drummond, "In addition to the need to become lay lawyers and accountants when dealing with the government, firms also have to take on the role of being library scientists. If they are not prepared to do this, or if they don't have a team to do this they are not ready to get in the game."

"The more a firm learns about an agency and the more it can demonstrate that knowledge to agency officials, the more OSDBU staff will be positively disposed toward helping that firm." Encouraging OSDBU staff to go the extra mile for your firm is an objective. When the OSDBU works hand-in-hand with the PCR to set aside procurements for the 8(a)BD program that is going the extra mile in today's terms.

Sometimes when firms understand the mission of the agency and can propose an activity to meet a pressing demand, it may be possible to win a sole source procurement." Drummond notes. Federal Acquisition Regulations (FAR) on the matter are as follows:

6.302-1 Only one responsible source and no other supplies or services will satisfy agency requirements.

(a) Authority.
(1) Citations: <u>10 U.S.C. 2304(c)(1)</u> or <u>41 U.S.C. 253(c)(1)</u>.
(2) When the supplies or services required by the agency are available from only one responsible source, or, for DoD, NASA, and the Coast Guard, from only one or a limited number of responsible sources, and no other type of supplies or services will satisfy agency requirements, full and open competition need not be provided for.
(i) Supplies or services may be considered to be **available from only one source** if the source has submitted an unsolicited research proposal that—
(A) Demonstrates a **unique and innovative concept** (see definition at <u>2.101</u>), or, demonstrates a unique capability of the source to provide the particular research services proposed;
(B) **Offers a concept or services not otherwise available** to the Government; and
(C) Does not resemble the substance of a pending competitive acquisition. (See <u>10 U.S.C. 2304(d)(1)(A)</u> and <u>41 U.S.C. 253(d)(1)(A)</u>.)
(ii) Supplies may be deemed to be available only from the original source in the case of a follow-on contract

for the continued development or production of a major system or highly specialized equipment, including major components thereof, when it is likely that award to any other source would result in—

(A) Substantial duplication of cost to the Government that is not expected to be recovered through competition; or

(B) Unacceptable delays in fulfilling the agency's requirements. (See 10 U.S.C. 2304(d)(1)(B) or 41 U.S.C. 253 (d)(1)(B).)

(iii) For DoD, NASA, and the Coast Guard, services may be deemed to be available only from the original source in the case of follow-on contracts for the continued provision of highly specialized services when it is likely that award to any other source would result in—

(A) Substantial duplication of cost to the Government that is not expected to be recovered through competition; or

(B) Unacceptable delays in fulfilling the agency's requirements. (See 10 U.S.C. 2304(d)(1)(B).)

(b) *Application.* This authority shall be used, if appropriate, in preference to the authority in 6.302-7; it shall not be used when any of the other circumstances is applicable. Use of this authority may be appropriate in situations such as the following (these examples are not intended to be all inclusive and do not constitute authority in and of themselves):

(1) When there is a reasonable basis to conclude that the agency's minimum needs can only be satisfied by—

(i) Unique supplies or services available from only one source or only one supplier with unique capabilities; or

(ii) For DoD, NASA, and the Coast Guard, unique supplies or services available from only one or a limited number of sources or from only one or a limited number of suppliers with unique capabilities.

(2) The existence of limited rights in data, patent rights, copyrights, or secret processes; the control of basic raw material; or similar circumstances, make the supplies and services available from only one source (however, the mere existence of such rights or circumstances does not in and of itself justify the use of these authorities) (see Part 27).

(3) When acquiring utility services (see 41.101), circumstances may dictate that only one supplier can furnish the service (see 41.202); or when the contemplated contract is for construction of a part of a utility system and

the utility company itself is the only source available to work on the system.

(4) When the agency head has determined in accordance with the agency's standardization program that only specified makes and models of technical equipment and parts will satisfy the agency's needs for additional units or replacement items, and only one source is available.

(c) *Application for brand name descriptions.* An acquisition that uses a brand name description or other purchase description to specify a particular brand name, product, or feature of a product, peculiar to one manufacturer does not provide for full and open competition regardless of the number of sources solicited. It shall be justified and approved in accordance with FAR 6.303 and 6.304. The justification should indicate that the use of such descriptions in the acquisition is essential to the Government's requirements, thereby precluding consideration of a product manufactured by another company. See 5.102(a)(6) for the requirement to post the brand name justification. (Brand-name or equal descriptions, and other purchase descriptions that permit prospective contractors to offer products other than those specifically referenced by brand name, provide for full and open competition and do not require justifications and approvals to support their use.)

(d) Limitations.

(1) Contracts awarded using this authority shall be supported by the written justifications and approvals described in 6.303 and 6.304.

(2) For contracts awarded using this authority, the notices required by 5.201 shall have been published and any bids and proposals must have been considered.

The current USAID OSDBU Director, Maurico Vera, suggests that sole sourcing is a difficult sell. His advice to 8(a)BD firms is to concentrate on opportunities that have already been identified. "There's plenty out there already without trying to enter the very tough battlefield of the sole source domain." A budget has already been allocated for "real live" opportunities. Going after the "live ones," according to Vera, is a better use of valuable time and resources. Vera also advises firms to develop a niche and concentrate in target areas. It's not credible to claim that you can do it all. Based on the experience of meeting so many small business owners, OSDBU officers and other agency staff can sense when a firm is overstating its experience and capabilities.

Although OSDBUs can be a useful resource to help 8(a)BD firms understand and make inroads into the federal procurements of agencies, it's up to 8(a)BD firm owners to know how to interact with them in order to get the most out of the situation. As Verl Zanders underscored in his foreword, there's a human element in everything. It's only natural to pay more attention to those who stand out and distinguish themselves as worthy knowledgeable competitors.

While understanding the rules for engaging in federal government contracting is crucial, at the end of the day nothing is more important than understanding that *"people buy from people."*

As the successful graduates profiled in the first *"Gems of Wisdom"* book underscored, to get ahead and to be successful both while in the program and after graduation, people have to like you. Whether located in an OSDBU office, a program office, or in a contracts office, the staff must like you in order to help you to the maximum extent within their power.

Perhaps the most important *gem of wisdom* to pass on is: "One must never forget the human touch in dealing with people."

An OSDBU Directory is presented at the end of this chapter.

Chapter Two imparts *Gems of Wisdom* of Procurement Facilitators.

■ Defense Contract Management Agency (DCMA)

Website:
http://www.dcma.mil/DCMAHQ/dcma-sb/index.htm

Address:	Set up by Divisions
	(Contact office to obtain address)
Phone number:	Toll Free: (877) 662-3960
Director:	Acting Director: Ms. Mary A. Seabolt
	(703) 428-1130
	mary.seabolt@dcma.mil
Subcontracting Rep:	
	Ms. Margarette Trimble-Williams
	Comprehensive Subcontracting
	Division Chief
	(310) 900-6025
Mentor-Protégé Rep:	
	Ms. Elaine Howell Division Chief
	(675) 503-6369
Other:	Mr. Thomas Watkins
	East Division Chief
	(937) 656-3104
Other:	Ms. DeWillican Middleton
	(317) 510-2015

■ Defense Information Systems Agency (DISA)

Website:	http://www.disa.mil
Address:	701 S. Courthouse Road
	Office Code: D04, Room 1108-B
	Arlington, VA 22204-2199
Phone number:	(703) 607-6436
Fax number:	(703) 607-4173
Director:	Ms. Sharon Jones
	disasmallbusinessoffice@disa.mil
Deputy Director:	Mrs. Francisca Crouch
	disasmallbusinessoffice@disa.mil
Mentor-Protégé Rep:	
	Ms. Sharon Jones
	disasmallbusinessoffice@disa.mil

■ Defense Logistics Agency (DLA)

Website:	http://www.dla.mil/db/
Address:	8725 John J. Kingman Road
	DB Room 1127
	Fort Belvoir, VA 22060-6221
Phone number:	Primary: (703) 767- 0192, Alt:
	(703) 767- 1660
Fax number:	(703) 767-1670
Director:	Ms. Peg Meehan
	(703) 767- 1662
	peg.meehan@dla.mil
Deputy Director:	Ms. Diana Maykowskyj
	(703) 767-1656
	diana.maykowskyj@dla.mil
8(a)/SDB Rep:	Ms. Patricia Cleveland
	(703) 767-1652
	patricia.cleveland@dla.mil
WOSB Rep:	Ms. Patricia Cleveland
	(703) 767-1652

	patricia.cleveland@dla.mil
HUBZone Rep:	Ms. Peggy Glasheen
	(703) 767-1657
	peggy.glasheen@dla.mil
VO/SDVOSB Rep:	Ms. Peggy Glasheen
	(703) 767-1657
	peggy.glasheen@dla.mil
Subcontracting Rep:	Ms. Diana Maykowskyj
	(703) 767-1656
	diana.maykowskyj@dla.mil
Mentor-Protégé Rep:	Ms. Diana Maykowskyj
	(703) 767-1656
	diana.maykowskyj@dla.mil
HBCU/MI Rep:	Ms. Peggy Glasheen
	(703) 767-1657
	peggy.glasheen@dla.mil

■ Department of the Air Force

Website:	http://www.selltoairforce.org
Address:	901 North Stuart Street, Suite 802
	Arlington, VA 22203
Phone number:	(703) 696-1103
Fax number:	(703) 696-1170
Director:	Mr. Ronald A. Poussard
	(703) 696-1103
	ronald.poussard@pentagon.af.mil
Deputy Director:	Mr. John Caporal
	(703) 696-1103
	john.caporal@pentagon.af.mil
8(a)/SDB Rep:	Mary Reynolds
	(703) 696-1103
	mary.reynolds@pentagon.af.mil
WOSB Rep:	Sherry Freeman
	(703) 696-1103
	sherry.freeman@pentagon.af.mil
HUBZone Rep:	Sherry Freeman
	(703) 696-1103
	sherry.freeman@pentagon.af.mil
VO/SDVOSB Rep:	Ms. Terese Herston
	(703) 696-1103
	terese.herston@pentagon.af.mil
Subcontracting Rep:	Mary Reynolds
	(703) 696-1103
	mary.reynolds@pentagon.af.mil
Mentor-Protégé Rep:	Ms. Satheda Bush
	(210) 536-1317
	satheda.bush@brooks.af.mil
HBCU/MI Rep:	Dr. Alain Hunter
	(703) 696-1103
	alain.hunter@pentagon.af.mil
Other:	MTAPP
	Mr. Phil Roth
	(210) 536-1317
	phil.roth@brooks.af.mil
Other:	Native American/ Tribally Owned
	Small Business
	Sherry Freeman
	(703) 696-1103
	Sherry.freeman@pentagon.af.mil

■ Department of the Army

Website:	http://www.sellingtoarmy.info/
Address:	The Pentagon, Room 3B514
	Washington, DC 20310-0106
Phone number:	(703) 697-2868
Fax number:	(703) 693-3898
Director:	Tracey L. Pinson
Deputy Director:	Paul Gardner

■ Department of Defense

Website:	http://www.acq.osd.mil/osbp/
Address:	1777 North Kent Street, Suite 9100
	Washington, DC 22209
Phone number:	(703) 604-0157 ext. 151
Fax number:	(703) 588-7561
Director:	Anthony Martoccia

■ Department of Defense Education Activity (DoDEA)

Website:	http://www.dodea.edu/offices/
	procurement/index.cfm
Address:	4040 N. Fairfax Drive
	Arlington, VA 22203-1635
Phone number:	(703) 588-3713
Fax number:	(703) 588-3713
SB Comp. Advocate:	Marybeth Olexy
	(703) 588-3609
	Marybeth.olexy@hq.dodea.edu
SB Program Manager:	Nikki Burley
	(703) 588-3632
	nikki.burley@hq.dodea.edu
Alternate SB Program Manager:	Ray Robinson
	(703) 588-3626
	willie.robinson@hq.dodea.edu

■ Department of the Navy

Website:	http://www.donhq.navy.mil/OSBP
Address:	720 Kennon Street, SE
	Building 36, Room 207
	Washington, DC 20374-5015
Phone number:	(202) 685-6485
Fax number:	(202) 685-6865
Director:	Mr. Timothy Foreman
	(202) 685-6485
	timothy.foreman@navy.mil
Deputy Director:	Ms. Oreta Stinson
	(202) 685-6485
	oreta.stinson@navy.mil
8(a)/SDB Rep:	Ms. Patricia Obey
	(202) 685-6485
	patricia.obey@navy.mil
WOSB Rep:	Ms. Alyse Bullock
	(202) 685-6485
	alyse.bullock@navy.mil
HUBZone Rep:	Ms. Alyse Bullock
	(202) 685-6485
	alyse.bullock@navy.mil
VO/SDVOSB Rep:	Mr. Timothy Foreman
	(202) 685-6485
	timothy.foreman@navy.mil
Subcontracting Rep:	Ms. Patricia Obey
	(202) 685-6485
	mary.reynolds@pentagon.af.mil

Mentor-Protégé Rep:	Ms. Oreta Stinson
	(202) 685-6485
	oreta.stinson@navy.mil
HBCU/MI Rep:	Ms. Oreta Stinson
	(202) 685-6485
	oreta.stinson@navy.mil
Other:	Ms. Shawn Smith
	Program Analyst
	Technical Support
	(202) 685-6485
	shawn.smith4@navy.mil
Other:	Mr. Derrick Capers
	Administrative Assistant
	(202) 685-6485
	derrick.capers@navy.mil

■ Executive Office of the President

Website:	http://www.whitehouse.gov/omb/
Address:	725 17th Street, NW, Room 5001
	Washington, DC 20503
Phone number:	(202) 395-7669
Fax number:	(202) 395-3982
Director:	Althea A. Kireilis

■ Federal Deposit Insurance Corporation

Website:	http://www.fdic.gov/buying/goods/
	index.html
Address:	Virginia Square, L. William Seidman
	Center
	3501 Fairfax Drive, Room E2014
	Arlington, VA 22226
Phone number:	(703) 562-6070
Fax number:	(703) 562-6069
Director:	Mr. Robert Elcan
	Section Chief
	Minority Outreach Program
WOSB Rep:	Ms. Velda Fludd
	Minority Woman Outreach Spec
	(703) 562-6071

■ General Services Administration

Website:	http://www.gsa.gov/smallbusiness
Address:	1800 F Street, NW
	Washington, DC 20405
Phone number:	(202) 501-1021
Fax number:	(202) 208-5938
Associate Administrator:	Felipe Mendoza

■ National Aeronautics and Space Administration

Website:	http://www.osbp.nasa.gov/
Address:	NASA Office of Small Business
	Programs
	300 E Street, SW
	Washington, DC 20546-0001
Phone number:	(202) 358-2088
Fax number:	(202) 358-3261
Director:	Mr. Glenn A. Delgado
	Assistant Administrator
	(202) 358-2088
	smallbusiness@nasa.gov

SBIR/STTR:	Mr. Dave Grove
	(202) 358-2088
	smallbusiness@nasa.gov
8(a)/SDB Rep:	Dr. Eleanor Chiogioji
	(202) 358-2088
	smallbusiness@nasa.gov
WOSB Rep:	Dr. Eleanor Chiogioji
	(202) 358-2088
	smallbusiness@nasa.gov
HUBZone Rep:	Dr. Eleanor Chiogioji
	(202) 358-2088
	smallbusiness@nasa.gov
VO/SDVOSB Rep:	Mr. Dave Grove
	(202) 358-2088
	smallbusiness@nasa.gov
Subcontracting Rep:	Dr. Eleanor Chiogioji
	(202) 358-2088
	smallbusiness@nasa.gov
Mentor-Protégé Rep:	Mr. Dave Grove
	(202) 358-2088
	smallbusiness@nasa.gov
HBCU/MI Rep:	Dr. Eleanor Chiogioji
	(202) 358-2088
	smallbusiness@nasa.gov

■ National Science Foundation
Website: http://www.nsf.gov/
Address: 4201 Wilson Boulevard, Room 527
Arlington, VA, 22230
Phone number: (703) 292-7082
Fax number: (703) 292-9055
Director: Donald Senich

■ Nuclear Regulatory Commission
Website: http://www.nrc.gov/about-nrc/
overview.html
Address: Office of Small Business and Civil
Rights
11545 Rockville Pike, MS T2 F18
Rockville, MD 20852
Phone number: (301) 415-7380
Fax number: (301) 415-5953
Director: Corenthis B. Kelley
SB Program Manager: Mauricio P. Vera
Smithsonian Institution
Website: http://www.si.edu/oeema/sdbu.htm
Address: Office of Equal Employment and
Minority Affairs
600 Maryland Avenue SW
Suite 2091 MRC 521
Washington, DC 20024
Phone number: (202) 633-6430
Fax number: (202) 633-6427
Director: Era L. Marshall
SD Program Manager: Rudy D. Watley

■ Social Security Administration
Website: http://www.socialsecurity.gov/oag/
osdbu/osdbu.htm
Address: 7111 Security Blvd
1st Floor, Rear Entrance
Baltimore, MD 21244

Phone number: (410) 965-7467
Fax number: (410) 965-2965
Director: Mr. Wayne McDonald
wayne.mcdonald@ssa.gov
SADBU Specialist: Ms. Patricia Bullock
(410) 965-9457
pat.bullock@ssa.gov

Transportation Security Administration
Website: http://www.tsa.gov/join/smallbiz/
index.shtm
Address: TSA HQ-West Building, 4th Floor,
TSA-14
601 S. 12th Street
Arlington, VA 22202
Phone number: (571) 227-2070
Program Manager: Ramona Jones

■ U.S. Agency for International Development
Website: http://www.usaid.gov/business/small_
business/
Address: Ronald Reagan Building, USAID/
OSDBU/MRC
1300 Pennsylvania Ave., NW
Room 5.8C
Washington, DC 20523-5800
Phone number: (202) 712-1500
Fax number: (202) 216-3056
Director: Mauricio Vera

■ U.S. Department of Agriculture
Website: http://www.usda.gov/da/smallbus/
Address: 1400 Independence Avenue, SW.
AG STOP 9501, Room 1085, South
Building
Washington, DC 20250-9501
Phone number: (202) 720-7117
Fax number: (202) 720-3001
Director: Jim House
JamesE.House@usda.gov
Deputy Director: Joe Ware
Joe.Ware@usda.gov
Associate Director: Barbara LaCour
Barbara.LaCour@usda.gov
Associate Director: Belinda Ward
Belinda.Ward@usda.gov
WOSB Rep: Sherry Cohen
SherryR.Cohen@usda.gov
VO/SDVOSB Rep: Linda Epstein
Linda.Epstein@usda.gov
Subcontracting Rep: Sherry Cohen
SherryR.Cohen@usda.gov
Procurement Forecast:
Michael Spencer
Michael.Spencer@usda.gov
Vendor Outreach Program:
Janet Baylor
Janet.Baylor@usda.gov
First Tuesday Association Breakfast Briefing:
Roxanne Lane
Roxanne.Lane@usda.gov

8(a)/SDB Program: Debra Lucas
                    Debra.Lucas@usda.gov
AbilityOne Program: Lisa Brown
                    LisaM.Brow@usda.gov

■ **U.S. Department of Commerce**
Website: http://www.osec.doc.gov/osdbu/
Address: 14th & Constitution Avenue, NW
                    Room H-6411
                    Washington, DC 20230
Phone number: (202) 482-1472
Fax number: (202) 482-0501
Director: La Juene Desmukes

■ **U.S. Department of Education**
Website: http://www.ed.gov/about/offices/list/
                    ods/osdbu.html
Address: Potomac Center Plaza, Room 7050
                    550 12th St. SW
                    Washington, DC 20202
Phone number: (202) 245-6300
Fax number: (202) 245-6304
E-mail: small.business@ed.gov
Director: Dr. Kristi Wilson Hill
                    (202) 245-6300
                    Kristi.Wilson@ed.gov
8(a)/SDB Rep: Ms. Marcella Coverson
                    (202) 245-6300
                    Marcella.Coverson@ed.gov
WOSB Rep: Ms. Melanie Carter
                    (202) 245-6300
                    Melanie.Carter@ed.gov
HUBZone Rep: Ms. Marcella Coverson
                    (202) 245-6300
                    Marcella.Coverson@ed.gov
VO/SDVOSB Rep: Mr. Howard Willis
                    (202) 245-6300
                    Howard.Willis@ed.gov

■ **U.S. Department of Energy**
Website: http://smallbusiness.doe.gov/
                    index.html
Address: 1000 Independence Avenue, S.W.
                    Room # 5B-148
                    Washington, DC 20585
Phone number: (202) 586-7377
Fax number: (202) 586-5488
Director: Ms. Theresa Alvillar-Speake
                    (202) 586-8383
Associate Director: Ms. Adrienne Cisneros
                    (202) 586-7951
Special Assistant to OSDBU Director:
                    Mr. Lee Avila
                    (202) 586-3993
                    Lee.Avila@hq.doe.gov
Program Manager
                    (Business and Community
                    Development):
                    Mr. Sterling Nichols
                    (202) 586-8698
                    Sterling.Nichols@hq.doe.gov

Procurement Analyst:Ms. Brenda Degraffenreid
                    (202) 586-4620
                    Brenda.Degraffenreid@hq.doe.gov
Procurement Analyst:Mr. Nickolas Demer
                    (202) 586-1614
                    Nickolas.Demer@hq.doe.gov
Small Business Analyst:
                    Ms. Rita Martinez Solon
                    (202) 586-0654
                    Rita.Solon@hq.doe.gov

■ **U.S. Department of Health and Human Services**
Website: http://www.hhs.gov/osdbu/
Address: 200 Independence Avenue, S.W.
                    Room 360G – Hubert H. Humphrey
                    Building
                    Washington, DC 20201
Phone number: (202) 690-7300
Fax number: (202) 260-4872
Director: Debbie Ridgley
                    (202) 690-7300
                    Debbie.Ridgely@HHS.Gov
Senior Advisor: Clarence Randall
                    (202) 690-8544
                    Clarence.Randall@HHS.Gov
8(a)/SDB Rep: Teneshia G. Alston
                    Small Business Analyst
                    (202) 205-4919
                    Teneshia.Alston@HHS.Gov
WOSB Rep: Teneshia G. Alston
                    Small Business Analyst
                    (202) 205-4919
                    Teneshia.Alston@HHS.Gov
HUBZone Rep: Debra Peters
                    Small Business Analyst
                    (202) 690-8457
                    Debra.Peters@HHS.Gov
VO/SDVOSB Rep: Debra Peters
                    Small Business Analyst
                    (202) 690-8457
                    Debra.Peters@HHS.Gov
Subcontracting Rep: Teneshia G. Alston
                    Small Business Analyst
                    (202) 205-4919
                    Teneshia.Alston@HHS.Gov
Mentor-Protégé Rep: Teneshia G. Alston
                    Small Business Analyst
                    (202) 205-4919
                    Teneshia.Alston@HHS.Gov
HBCU/MI Rep: Teneshia G. Alston
                    (202) 205-4919
                    Teneshia.Alston@HHS.Gov
Program Analyst: Ms. Linda M. Purnell
                    (202) 690-7302
                    linda.purnell@hhs.gov
Program Support Analyst:
                    Ms. Ruth E. Lewis
                    (202) 690-7301
                    ruth.lewis@hhs.gov

HHS Small Business Specialists
AHRQ: Vivian Kim
(240) 276-1017
Vivian.Kim@samhsa.hhs.gov
CDC: Curtis Bryant (Team Leader)
(770) 488-2806
cbryant1@cdc.gov
CMS: Alice P. Roache
(410) 786-9319
alice.roache@cms.hhs.gov
FDA: Douglas Smith
(301) 827-1994
douglas.smith@fda.hhs.gov
HRSA: Douglas Smith
(301) 443-6678
DSmith@HRSA.Gov
IHS: Nelia "Kay" Holder
(301) 443-1480
nelia.holder@ihs.gov
NIH: Jonathan Ferguson
(301) 496-9639
njf27t@nih.gov
NIH: Barbara Hall
(301) 496-9639
hallba@od.nih.gov
NIH: Annette Owens-Scarboro (Team
Leader)
(301) 496-9639
scarbora@od.nih.gov
PSC: Anita Allen
(301) 443-1715
Anita.Allen@PSC.hhs.gov
SAMSHA: Vivian Kim
(240) 276-1017
Vivian.Kim@samhsa.hhs.gov

■ **U.S. Department of Homeland Security**
Website: http://www.dhs.gov/openforbusiness
Address: Mailing Address:
Department of Homeland Security
245 Murray Dr. SW, Bldg. 410 Room
3124-A
Washington, DC 20528
Physical Address:
7th & D Street SW
Washington, DC 20004
Phone number: (202) 447-5555
Fax number: (202) 447-5552
Director: Mr. Kevin Boshears
WOSB Reps: Ms. Wendy Hill
(202) 447-5286
wendy.hill@dhs.gov
Ms. Ilene Waggoner
(202)447-5282
ilene.waggoner@dhs.gov
VO/SDVOSB Rep: Mr. Dan Sturdivant
(202) 447-5289
dan.sturdivant@dhs.gov
Subcontracting Rep: Mr. Kyle Groome
(202) 447-5281
kyle.groome@dhs.gov

Mentor-Protégé Rep: Ms. Angela Williams
(202) 447-5280
angela.williams1@dhs.gov

■ **U.S. Department of Housing and Urban Development**
Website: http://www.hud.gov/offices/osdbu/
index.cfm
Address: 451 7th Street, SW
Room 10156
Washington, DC 20410-1000
Phone number: (202) 708-1428
Fax number: (202) 708-7642
Acting Director: Ms. Valerie Hayes
8(a)/SDB Rep: Ms. Arnette McGill-Moore
WOSB Rep: Ms. Meishoma Hayes
HUBZone Rep: Ms. Meishoma Hayes
VO/SDVOSB Rep: Ms. Ozema Moore
Subcontracting Rep: Ms. Ozema Moore

■ **U.S. Department of the Interior**
Website: http://www.doi.gov/osdbu/
Address: 1849 C Street, NW
MS2252 MIB
Washington, D.C. 20240
Phone number: (202) 208-3493
Fax number: (202) 208-7444
E-mail: DOI_OSDBU@iosl.doi.gov
Director: Mr. Mark Oliver
(202) 208-3493
mark_oliver@ios.doi.gov
Deputy Director: Mr. Gary Wade
(202) 208-3493
gary_wade@ios.doi.gov

■ **U.S. Department of Justice**
Website: http://www.usdoj.gov/jmd/osdbu/
Address: 1331 Pennsylvania Avenue, NW
National Place Building, Suite 1010
Washington, DC 20530
Phone number: Primary: (202) 616-0523
Toll Free: (800) 345-3712
Fax number: (202) 616-1717
Director: Mr. David Sutton
(202) 616-0523
david.sutton@usdoj.gov

■ **U.S. Department of Labor**
Website: http://www.dol.gov/osbp/
welcome.htm
Address: 200 Constitution Avenue, NW
Room C-2318
Washington, DC 20210
Phone number: (202) 693-6460
Fax number: (202) 693-6485
Director: Jose Lira

■ U.S. Department of State

Website:	http://www.state.gov/m/a/sdbu/
Address:	SA-6
	Room L500
	Washington, DC 20522
Phone number:	(703) 875-6822
Fax number:	(703) 875-6825
Director:	Gregory Mayberry
Women Business Rep:	
	Patricia Culbreth
HUBZone Advocate:	Judith Thomas
Veteran Business Advocate:	
	Willie Taylor

■ U.S. Department of Transportation

Website:	http://www.osdbu.dot.gov/
Address:	1200 New Jersey Avenue, SE
	Washington, DC 20590
Phone number:	(202) 366-1930
Fax number:	(202) 366-7228
Director:	Ms. Denise Rodriguez-Lopez
Deputy Director:	Mr. Leonardo San Roman
WOSB Rep:	Ms. Pat Hodge
	pat.hodge@dot.gov
VO/SDVOSB Rep:	Ms. Pat Hodge
	pat.hodge@dot.gov
Other:	National Information Clearinghouse
	(800) 532-1169

■ U.S. Department of the Treasury

Website:	http://www.treas.gov/offices/
	management/dcfo/osdbu/
Address:	1500 Pennsylvania Ave., NW
	Mail Code: 655 15th/6099
	Washington, DC 20220
Phone number:	(202) 622-0530
Fax number:	(202) 622-4963
Director:	Virginia Bellamy-Graham
	(202) 622-2826
Women Business Rep:	
	Renee Fitzgerald
	(202) 622-0793

■ U.S. Department of Veterans Affairs

Website:	http://www.va.gov/OSDBU/
Address:	810 Vermont Avenue, NW
	Washington, DC 20420
Phone number:	(202) 461-4300
Fax number:	(202) 461-4301
Director:	Mr. Scott Denniston
	scott.denniston@va.gov
Deputy Director:	Mr. Wayne Simpson
	wayne.simpson@va.gov
Subcontracting Reps:	Mr. Mark Taylor
	(202) 461-4256
Ms. Lynette Simmons	
	(202) 461-4258
Sr Procurement Specialist:	
	Ms. Deborah Van Dover
	(202) 461-4255

VA Small Business Specialists

Bundling:	Ms. Victoria Johnson
	(202) 641-4253
Bundling:	Mr. Cordell Smith
	(202) 641-4260
Outreach:	Ms. Linda Sitney
	(202) 461-4262
Outreach:	Ms. Tamika Gray
	(202) 461-4263

■ U.S. Environmental Protection Agency

Website:	http://www.epa.gov/osdbu/
Address:	1200 Pennsylvania Avenue, NW
	Mail Code 1230T
	Washington, DC 20460
Phone number:	(202) 566-2075
Fax number:	(202) 566-0266
Director:	Jeanette L. Brown

■ U.S. Postal Service

Website:	http://www.usps.com/purchasing/
	supplierdiversity/
	diversitymenu.htm
Address:	475 L'Enfant Plaza SW
	Room 4430
	Washington, DC 20260-6204
Phone number:	(202) 268-4633
Fax number:	(202) 268-4012
Manager Supplier Diversity:	
	Janice Williams-Hopkins

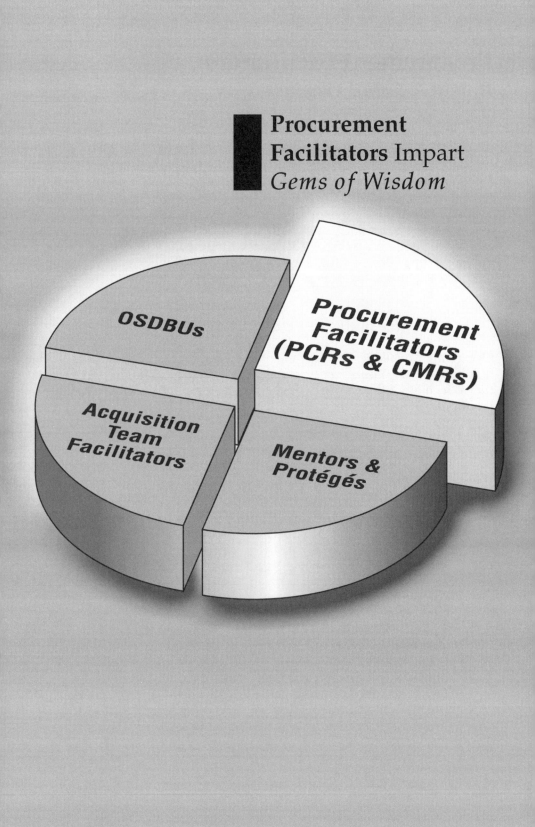

Procurement Facilitators Impart Gems of Wisdom

OSDBUs

Procurement Facilitators (PCRs & CMRs)

Acquisition Team Facilitators

Mentors & Protégés

Procurement Facilitators
Impart *Gems of Wisdom*

Knowledge is power! Its axiomatic that a knowledgeable 8(a)BD firm owner is more competitive than a less knowledgeable one.

It's important for 8(a)BD firm owners to be knowledgeable about the entire network of business development resources, not just about a portion of it. Conferring with and taking advantage of the business development assistance rendered by SBA's Business Opportunity Specialist (BOS) is only a starting place. Doing the same with the OSDBUs is another step in the process of knowledge acquisition.

Utilizing the assistance of Procurement Center Representatives and Commercial Marketing Representatives completes the picture.

One *gem of wisdom* that was gleaned from successful graduates in the first book in the "*Gems*" series is that they were successful in part because they effectively utilized every business development resource available to them.

Simply put, PCRs and CMRs are additional business development resources. In a nutshell, the role they play is as follows:

> **PCR - Procurement Center Representatives** - increase the small business share of Federal procurement awards by initiating small business set-asides, reserving procurements for competition among small business firms, providing small business sources to Federal buying activities, and counseling small firms. In addition, PCRs, advocate for the breakout of items for full and open competition to affect savings to the Federal Government.

> **CMR - Commercial Marketing Representatives** - are stationed in area offices, conduct compliance reviews of prime contractors, counsel small businesses on how to obtain subcontracts, conduct matchmaking activities to facilitate subcontracting to small business, and provide orientation and training on the Subcontracting Assistance Program for both large and small businesses.

PCRs: Getting a Piece of Prime Contract Action

One of the most powerful resources the U.S. Small Business Administration has to promote the inclusion of small firms in federal procurements is its Procurement Center Representatives (PCRs). What do they do exactly?

Procurement Center Representatives (PCRs) work with federal agencies and procuring activities by reviewing proposed acquisitions to determine whether they can be set aside for small businesses. If the PCR believes that the agency/activity should set aside the procurement for small business, the PCR may issue a formal request to the contracting officer. Should the contracting officer reject the PCR's recommendation, the PCR may appeal the rejection to the Head Contracting Authority (HCA) for the agency/activity.

Verl Zanders, former PCR and OSDBU official, provides a "reality check" on what happens in practice.

The first thing to understand, according to Zanders, is that SBA employs PCRs; they are not employed by the agencies in which they work. This is important. By contrast, OSDBU staff are employed by the agencies in which they work.

As a PCR, Zanders viewed himself as an independent advocate and took pride in battling with the agencies on behalf of 8(a)s. But here's the thing: Because agencies often receive their funds a few months after the fiscal year has already started, and because all of the funds cannot be spent during the last couple of months in a fiscal year, there are only a few months left to obligate agency funds. Thus, although PCRs can theoretically hold up a procurement, agencies can also make a case that holding up the procurement is not in the best interest of the agency as a whole.

In taking up any battle, one's weapons have to be sharp. Zanders notes that he always checked out the 8(a)BD firm to be certain that the firm "had the goods." He performed the necessary due diligence on the firm so that when he entered battle with the agencies on their behalf, he knew he had solid 8(a)BD firms on whose behalf he was advocating.

As stated earlier, there is a human element in everything. Zanders had a passion for increasing the percentage of 8(a)BD and other small businesses that participated in agency procurements. He went the extra mile to make it happen. Today, while it's arguable how many PCRs and OSDBU staff are going the extra mile to fight for 8(a)BD firms, one thing is clear: If they do go the extra mile it will be for those 8(a)BD firms that are themselves going the extra mile to be the best they can be.

Rules that govern how PCRs function are set forth in Federal Acquisition Regulations (FAR), shown in Box 2.

Box 2:
FAR 19.402 Small Business Administration Procurement Center Representatives

(a)(1) The SBA may assign one or more procurement center representatives to any contracting activity or contract administration office to carry out SBA policies and programs. Assigned SBA procurement center representatives are required to comply with the contracting agency's directives governing the conduct of contracting personnel and the release of contract information. The SBA must obtain for its procurement center representatives security clearances required by the contracting agency.

(2) If a SBA procurement center representative is not assigned to the procuring activity or contract administration office, contact the SBA Office of Government Contracting Area Office serving the area in which the procuring activity is located for assistance in carrying out SBA policies and programs. See *http://www.sba.gov/GC/pcr.html* for the location of the SBA office servicing the activity.

(b) Upon their request and subject to applicable acquisition and security regulations, contracting officers shall give SBA procurement center representatives (or, if a procurement center representative is not assigned, see paragraph (a) of this section) access to all reasonably obtainable contract information that is directly pertinent to their official duties.

(c) The duties assigned by SBA to its procurement center representatives include the following:
(1) Reviewing proposed acquisitions to recommend—
    (i) The setting aside of selected acquisitions not unilaterally set aside by the contracting officer,
    (ii) New qualified small, veteran-owned small, service-disabled veteran-owned small, HUBZone small, small disadvantaged, and women-owned small business sources, and
    (iii) Breakout of components for competitive acquisitions.

(2) Reviewing proposed acquisition packages provided in accordance with 19.202-1(e). If the SBA procurement center representative (or, if a procurement center representative is not assigned, see paragraph (a) of this section) believes that the acquisition, as proposed, makes it unlikely that small businesses can compete for the prime contract, the representative shall recommend any alternate contracting method that the representative reasonably believes will increase small business prime contracting opportunities. The recommendation

---

shall be made to the contracting officer within 15 days after receipt of the package.

(3) **Recommending concerns for inclusion on a list of concerns to be solicited in a specific acquisition**.

(4) Appealing to the chief of the contracting office any contracting officer's determination not to solicit a concern recommended by the SBA for a particular acquisition, when not doing so results in no small business being solicited.

(5) Conducting periodic reviews of the contracting activity to which assigned to ascertain whether it is complying with the small business policies in this regulation.

(6) Sponsoring and participating in conferences and training designed to increase small business participation in the contracting activities of the office.

In addition to the foregoing, SBA has designated *breakout procurement center representatives* to address sustantial agency purchases. FAR rules shown in Box 3 govern the activities of the breakout procurement center representatives.

Box 3:
FAR 19.403 Small Business Administration Breakout Procurement Center Representative

(a) The SBA is required by section 403 of Pub. L. 98-577 to assign a breakout procurement center representative to each major procurement center. A major procurement center means a procurement center that, in the opinion of the administrator, purchases substantial dollar amounts of other than commercial items, and which has the potential to incur significant savings as a result of the placement of a breakout procurement representative.

The SBA breakout procurement center representative is an advocate for (1) the appropriate use of full and open competition, and (2) the breakout of items, when appropriate and while maintaining the integrity of the system in which such items are used. The SBA breakout procurement center representative is in addition to the SBA procurement center representative (see 19.402). When an SBA breakout procurement center representative is assigned, the SBA is required to assign at least two collocated small business technical advisors. Assigned SBA breakout procurement center representatives and technical advisors are required to comply with the contracting agency's directives governing the conduct of contracting personnel and the release of contract information. The SBA must obtain for its breakout procurement center representatives and technical advisors security clearances required by the contracting agency.

(b) Contracting officers shall comply with 19.402(b) in their relationships with SBA breakout procurement center representatives and SBA small business technical advisors.

(c) The SBA breakout procurement center representative is authorized to—

(1) Attend any provisioning conference or similar evaluation session during which determinations are made as to whether requirements are to be acquired using other than full and open competition and make recommendations with respect to such requirements to the members of such conference or session;

(2) Review, at any time, restrictions on competition previously imposed on items through acquisition method coding or similar procedures and recommend to personnel of the appropriate activity the prompt reevaluation of such limitations;

(3) Review restrictions on competition arising out of restrictions on the rights of the United States in technical data and, when appropriate, recommend that personnel of the appropriate activity initiate a review of the validity of such an asserted restriction;

(4) Obtain from any governmental source, and make available to personnel of the appropriate center, technical data necessary for the preparation of a competitive solicitation package for any item of supply or service previously acquired noncompetitively due to the unavailability of such technical data;

(5) Have access to procurement records and other data of the procurement center commensurate with the level of such representative's approved security clearance classification;

(6) Receive unsolicited engineering proposals and, when appropriate—

(i) Conduct a value analysis of such proposal to determine whether it, if adopted, will result in lower costs to the United States without substantially impeding legitimate acquisition objectives and forward to personnel of the appropriate center recommendations with respect to such proposal; or

(ii) Forward such proposals without analysis to personnel of the center responsible for reviewing them who shall furnish the breakout procurement center representative with information regarding the proposal's disposition;

(7) Review the systems that account for the acquisition and management of technical data within the procurement center to ensure that such systems provide the maximum availability and access to data needed for the preparation of offers to sell to the United States those supplies to which such data pertain which potential offerors are entitled to receive;

(8) Appeal the failure by the procurement center to act favorably on any recommendation made pursuant to paragraphs (c)(1) through (7) of this section. Such appeal must be in writing and shall be filed and processed in accordance with the appeal procedures set out at 19.505;

(9) Conduct familiarization sessions for contracting officers and other appropriate personnel of the procurement center to which assigned. Such sessions shall acquaint the participants with the duties and objectives of the representative and shall instruct them in the methods designed to further the breakout of items for procurement through full and open competition; and

(10) Prepare and personally deliver an annual briefing and report to the head of the procurement center to which assigned. Such briefing and report shall

detail the past and planned activities of the representative and shall contain recommendations for improvement in the operation of the center as may be appropriate. The head of such center shall personally receive the briefing and report and shall, within 60 calendar days after receipt, respond, in writing, to each recommendation made by the representative.

(d) The duties of the SBA small business technical advisors are to assist the SBA breakout procurement center representative in carrying out the activities described in paragraphs (c)(1) through (7) of this section to assist the SBA procurement center representatives (see FAR 19.402).

The foregoing demonstrates the importance of PCRs to the 8(a)BD program and to the business development prospects of 8(a) firms, in theory. To evaluate what happens in practice, 8(a)BD firms may want to ascertain:

- How many PCR-recommended small business set-asides have there been in a given agency in a given period of time?

- What percentage of the set-aside recommendations was accepted by contracting officers in the respective agency?

- How many of the rejected set-asides were appealed, successfully and unsuccessfully by the SBA?

- How many of the rejected set-asides were appealed at the highest level in a given agency, successfully and unsuccessfully?

- How many of the set-asides were initiated by the PCRs rather than by the Contracting Officers?

Answers to these questions will provide a realistic gauge on how aggressive and effective PCRs are in advocating for 8(a)s.

Arguably there are fewer 8(a) set-aside opportunities as time goes on because of the increasing size of individual federal procurements and contract bundling.

Contract bundling represents both a threat and an opportunity for some 8(a)BD firms. Opportunities under such circumstances are mostly associated with subcontracting, however. An overview of contract bundling is given below.

What is Contract Bundling?

The Small Business Reauthorization Act of 1997 defines contract bundling as "consolidating two or more procurement requirements for goods or services previously provided or performed under separate, smaller contracts into a solicitation of offers for a single contract that is unlikely to be suitable for award to a small business concern." The Act lists several factors that might cause unsuitability for award to a small business, including:

■ The diversity, size, or specialized nature of the elements of the performance, specified as:
--The aggregate dollar value of the anticipated award;
--The geographical dispersion of contract performance sites; or

■ Any combination of these criteria.

The Act requires each federal department and agency, to the maximum extent practicable, to: (1) structure contracting requirements to facilitate competition by and among small business concerns, taking all reasonable steps to eliminate obstacles to their participation; and (2) avoid unnecessary and unjustified bundling of contract requirements that may preclude small business participation in procurements as prime contractors.

Prior to bundling any contracts, agencies are required to conduct market research to determine whether contract bundling is necessary and justified. To justify contract bundling, agencies must demonstrate "measurably substantial benefits," such as cost savings, quality improvements, reduction in acquisition cycle times, or better terms and conditions. The Small Business Administration's implementing regulations further define "measurably substantial benefits" by requiring agencies to demonstrate:

■ For contracts of $75 million or less - - benefits equivalent to 10 percent of contract value (including options), or

■ For contracts over $75 million - - benefits equivalent to 5 percent of contract value (including options) or $7.5 million, whichever is greater.

Several provisions of the Federal Acquisition Regulation (FAR) establish responsibilities for agency personnel who are considering contract bundling. The FAR places responsibility on agency acquisition planners to structure requirements, to the maximum extent practicable, to facilitate competition by and among small business concerns, and avoid unnecessary and unjustified bundling. Agency contracting officers are required to: (1) perform market research to determine whether bundling is necessary and justified; (2) justify their determinations in acquisition strategy documentation that identifies measurably substantial benefits that meet the statutory and regulatory requirements; and (3) consult with SBA representatives on their acquisition strategies.

Why Are Contracts Bundled?

Increased demands to make the acquisition process quicker and less complex coupled with reductions in the overall acquisition workforce have driven acquisition managers to bundle requirements. To meet these demands agencies have increasingly consolidated contractual requirements into larger contracts and used limited and simplified competition procedures for acquiring products and services.

What is the Impact of Contract Bundling on Small Businesses?

According to a report prepared for SBA's Office of Advocacy (2001), for every 100 "bundled" contracts, 106 individual contracts are no longer available to small businesses. For every $100 awarded on a "bundled" contract, there is a $33 decrease to small businesses. Because these types of contracts "run longer and encompass a greater scope, competition is reduced in terms of frequency and the number of opportunities." Analysis of the data indicates that, even though the overall dollars spent in contracting with small businesses remained relatively constant, there has been a sharp overall decline in new contract awards. As of 2001, data showed a decline in new contract awards (i.e., new contracts rather than contract modifications or orders under existing contracts), from a high of 86,243 in fiscal year 1991 to a low of 34,261 in fiscal year 2001.

This harsh reality underscores the importance of being competitive. For 8(a)BD firms to thrive in today's federal marketplace they must use every resource at their disposal to increase their competitiveness.

Knowledge is itself a resource. The more of it an 8(a)BD firm owner possesses, the better off that firm will be and the better positioned it will be to effectively utilize resources. It's important to thoroughly understand how the system works and how acquisitions are selected for the 8(a) program. Accordingly, FAR rules that govern how such acquisitions are selected are shown in Box 4.

Box 4:
FAR 19.803 Selecting Acquisitions for the 8(a) Program

Through their cooperative efforts, the SBA and an agency match the agency's requirements with the capabilities of 8(a) concerns to establish a basis for the agency to contract with the SBA under the program. Selection is initiated in one of three ways:

(a) **The SBA advises an agency contracting activity through a search letter of an 8(a) firm's capabilities** and asks the agency to identify acquisitions to support the firm's business plans. In these instances, the SBA will provide at least the following information in order to enable the agency to match an acquisition to the firm's capabilities:

(1) Identification of the concern and its owners.
(2) Background information on the concern, including any and all information pertaining to the concern's technical ability and capacity to perform.
(3) The firm's present production capacity and related facilities.
(4) The extent to which contracting assistance is needed in the present and the future, described in terms that will enable the agency to relate the concern's plans to present and future agency requirements.
(5) If construction is involved, the request shall also include the following:
(i) The concern's capabilities in and qualifications for accomplishing various categories of maintenance, repair, alteration, and construction work in specific categories such as mechanical, electrical, heating and air conditioning, demolition, building, painting, paving, earth work, waterfront work, and general construction work.
(ii) The concern's capacity in each construction category in terms of estimated dollar value (*e.g.,* electrical, up to $100,000).

(b) **The SBA identifies a specific requirement for a particular 8(a) firm or firms and asks the agency contracting activity to offer the acquisition to the 8(a) Program for the firm(s).** In these instances, in addition to the information in paragraph (a) of this section, the SBA will provide—
(1) A clear identification of the acquisition sought; *e.g.,* project name or number;
(2) A statement as to how any additional needed equipment and real property will be provided in order to ensure that the firm will be fully capable of satisfying the agency's requirements;
(3) If construction, information as to the bonding capability of the firm(s); and
(4) Either—
(i) **If sole source request—**
(A) The reasons why the firm is considered suitable for this particular acquisition; *e.g.,* previous contracts for the same or similar supply or service; and

---

> (B) A statement that the firm is eligible in terms of NAICS code, business support levels, and business activity targets; or
>
> (ii) If competitive, a statement that at least two 8(a) firms are considered capable of satisfying the agency's requirements and a statement that the firms are also eligible in terms of the NAICS code, business support levels, and business activity targets. If requested by the contracting activity, SBA will identify at least two such firms and provide information concerning the firms' capabilities.
>
> (c) Agencies may also review other proposed acquisitions for the purpose of identifying requirements which may be offered to the SBA. Where agencies independently, or through the self marketing efforts of an 8(a) firm, identify a requirement for the 8(a) Program, they may offer on behalf of a specific 8(a) firm, for the 8(a) Program in general, or for 8(a) competition (see 19.800(e).

How To Take Advantage of the PCR Resource

Understanding what PCRs do and what questions to ask them to take advantage of their assistance is key.

The answer to that question varies according to which PCR you ask. The reason why the answer varies is because the agencies PCRs are working in vary, as do the procurements they are targeting. Take for example PCRs that focus on manufacturing contracts. In certain cases it may not be appropriate to request an 8(a) set-aside if there is no evidence that 8(a) firms are supplying parts that are called for in a manufacturer's specifications, for instance. PCRs that are targeting service-based contracts have a different set of considerations, however.

An important issue is raised through this example: The issue of the PCR's knowledge of the capability of 8(a)s. In conducting market analyses to ascertain whether there are any 8(a) firms that are qualified to perform the procurement, PCRs often turn to the Central Contract Registry (CCR) or to PRO-NET. This is one of the reasons why it's important to be registered on as many databases as possible.

While there are some general guidelines suggested below, it's clear that there's no substitute for picking up the phone and asking them directly. Accordingly, a list of PCRs is presented at the end of this chapter. Questions you may wish to pose to them might include, for instance:

- ■ I know about a procurement that's about to hit the street, can you advocate to set it aside for the 8(a) program so that it doesn't go full and open?

- ■ I know about a procurement that's about to hit the street, can you advocate for setting the procurement aside for my firm?

- I know that you are not necessarily covering the agency in which I have an interest but could you please advocate with that agency to set aside an upcoming procurement that I know about either for the 8(a) program or for my firm?

The bottom line is this: PCRs are trying to monitor over 2,000 buying activities. They can't do it alone; 8(a)BD firm owners must help identify upcoming procurements and work hand-in-glove with both the OSDBUs and the PCRs to plot a strategy to get them set-aside.

PCRs are stationed where they get the biggest bang for the buck, at the larger buying agencies. This doesn't prohibit them from advocating for small set-asides in smaller agencies, however. But, in order to do so they need the help of the 8(a)BD firms to identify the opportunities and to be their eyes and ears in agencies in which they don't have a representative.

It's also important to remember that while PCRs advocate, they don't dictate. Oftentimes agencies take the lead in determining which procurements they are recommending for the 8(a) program. There are three levels of fights, starting with the contract officer, that PCRs can have to change their minds, but they don't always win the battle. Therefore, its wise for 8(a) firms to get to know program officers and contract officers to the extent they can in order to warm them up to the idea of setting aside procurements for the 8(a) program.

Each 8(a)BD firm owner is an Ambassador for the program. The better the firm's reputation is, the more receptive the acquisition team will be toward setting aside major procurements for the 8(a) program.

CMRs: Getting a Piece of the Subcontracting Action

As can be surmised from the foregoing, subcontracting on large federal contracts is becoming increasingly important to small businesses, principally because subcontracts may offer the most opportunities for these businesses to participate in federal procurement. The number of prime contracts is shrinking, and many prime contracts have become so large that small businesses find it difficult to compete for them. Moreover, the Small Business Administration (SBA) reported that dollars paid for subcontracts is a growing trend, having increased 40 percent from fiscal year 1993 through fiscal 2001 growing from $65 billion to $91.1 billion, for instance.

What is a Commercial Market Representative?

Commercial Marketing Representatives (CMRs) working for the Small Business Administration (SBA) promote small business subcontracting

The legislative authority for the Subcontracting Assistance Program is Section 8(d) of the Small Business Act (as amended by Public Law 95-507), enacted in 1978. Section 8(d) is codified at 15 U.S.C. 637(d). This legislation designated SBA as the principal Government Agency responsible for enforcing the provisions of the law pertaining to subcontracting requirements.

in two ways: They review prime contractors' compliance with the requirements of their subcontracting plans, and they market small businesses to prime contractors.

A Commercial Market Representative (CMR) is a specialist assigned to the Subcontracting Assistance Program (Public Law 95-507 Enacted in 1978) who is responsible for the following functions:

- Facilitating the matching of large prime contractors with small business concerns;

- Counseling large prime contractors on their responsibilities to maximize subcontracting opportunities for small business concerns;

- Instructing large prime contractors on identifying small business concerns by means of the Central Contractors Register (CCR), business matchmaking events, and other resources and tools;

- Counseling small business concerns on how to market themselves to large prime contractors;

- Maintaining a portfolio of large prime contractors and conducting Subcontracting Orientation and Assistance Reviews (SOARs); and,

- Conducting periodic reviews, including compliance reviews.

Background Information on How the CMR Program Works in Practice

In 2002, the GAO undertook a study of the CRM's role. The following information was provided in the report, which concluded that the CMR role needed to be strategically planned at assessed.

> The federal government encourages federal prime contractors' use of small businesses as subcontractors by requiring prime contractors to develop plans with stated goals for subcontracting to various types of small businesses. Federal regulations require a subcontracting plan for each contract or contract modification that exceeds $500,000 ($1 million for construction contracts) and has subcontracting possibilities.

The Subcontracting Assistance Program is SBA's vehicle for increasing the percentage of subcontract awards to small businesses and ensuring that small businesses have the maximum practicable opportunity to participate in the performance of federal government contracts. SBA's Office of Government Contracting (OGC) oversees this program. SBA/OGC has six Area Offices responsible for all prime contractors' subcontracting performance.

The program is implemented by CMRs, who promote small business subcontracting in two primary ways, as described in SBA regulations. First, CMRs review prime contractors' compliance with the requirements of their subcontracting plans. They conduct on-site compliance reviews at prime contractors' facilities and validate how well the prime contractors are implementing their subcontracting plans. They also conduct "desk reviews," which are reviews of relevant subcontracting reports that are submitted by prime contractors and completed without on-site visits.

Second, CMRs conduct various marketing activities, such as marketing small businesses to prime contractors or matching certain types of small business subcontractors with prime contractors. CMRs perform this "matchmaking" through both personal introductions and the use of Web-based tools that help to connect prime contractors and subcontractors.

CMRs also provide various educational activities (e.g., seminars and workshops) for prime contractors, subcontractors, and agency officials as part of their marketing activities. In describing the duties required of CMRs, SBA regulations do not place a relative order of importance on any of these responsibilities.

In addition, CMRs work on various SBA special initiatives as part of their marketing activities. For example, CMRs promote SBA's special 8(a) subcontracting initiative, which focuses on increasing the number of subcontracts to small disadvantaged businesses. CMRs also promote several special initiatives involving SBA's Procurement Marketing and Access Network (PRO-Net). PRO-Net is a web-based system that allows prime contractors to advertise potential subcontracting opportunities and small businesses to advertise their capabilities as subcontractors. CMRs install

PRO-Net access stations at large prime contractor sites and public libraries, and train interested businesses and agencies in the use of PRO-Net to match prime contractors and subcontractors. Finally, CMRs conduct special training for agencies and contractors on SBA's historically underutilized business zones (HUBZone) Empowerment Contracting Program, which encourages economic development in HUBZones.

SBA/OGC also employs other contract specialists, who focus on small businesses as prime contractors rather than subcontractors. These include Procurement Center Representatives (PCRs), size determination specialists, and Certificate of Competency (COC) specialists. PCRs work with agencies to determine whether it is appropriate for acquisitions not set aside for small businesses to be set aside. Size determination specialists determine whether a small business meets existing size standards for all procurement programs for which status as a small business is required. COC specialists review a contracting officer's determination that the small business in question is not competent to perform on a particular contract.

The foregoing clarifies the intended role and *modis operandi* of CMRs. The information below, from the GAO, clarifies the picture of the realities that have faced the CMR program overtime.

...Over the past few years, the CMR role has become part-time, and CMRs now usually have additional roles that often take priority. CMRs appear to spend slightly more time on marketing activities than on compliance monitoring, and they now rely much more frequently on desk reviews than on-site visits for the latter. In addition, workloads and prime contractor coverage vary greatly between CMRs...

At the end of fiscal year 2001, about 90 percent of the CMRs had other substantial responsibilities in addition to their CMR duties. At that time, only 4 of the 39 CMRs were full-time CMRs. The number of part-time CMRs has grown over time, increasing twelve-fold since 1992. (SBA officials anticipate the continued assignment of additional roles to CMRs and other contracting specialists.) In addition, despite the fact that a larger number of staff had CMR duties at the end of fiscal year 2001 than in fiscal 1992, the number of CMR fulltime equivalents (FTEs) declined 28 percent—from 25 to about 18—during this period.

Times change and fiscal realities and budgetary constraints change with the times. Wise 8(a)BD firm owners, as the successful graduates interviewed for the first "*Gems*" book conveyed, take the time to stay abreast of changes in the environment that have an impact on their business. Again, there is no substitute for picking up the phone and calling the nearest CMR to ascertain what they can do to help you today.

How To Take Advantage of the CMR Resource

Understanding the role that CMRs play, and knowing what questions are appropriate to ask them to take advantage of their assistance, is key?

Similarly as in the case of PCRs, the answer to that question varies according to which CMR you ask. While there are some general guidelines suggested below, it's also clear that there is no substitute for picking up the phone and asking them. Based on a discussion with CMRs there is really only one question to ask them, which is: Can you introduce me to a particular prime contractor and can you help me get my foot in the door?

What Are PTACs?

In addition to PCRs and CMRs, PTACs are yet another business development resource for 8(a)BD firms and other small businesses. Their role is to help firms understand the requirements of government contracting and to impart knowledge that helps small businesses successfully perform federal, state and local government contracts.

The Procurement Technical Assistance Program (PTAP) was authorized by Congress in 1985 in an effort to expand the number of businesses capable of participating in the Government Marketplace. Administered by the Department of Defense Defense Logistics Agency (DLA), the program provides matching funds through cooperative agreements with state and local governments and non-profit organizations for the establishment of Procurement Technical Assistance Centers (PTACs) to provide procurement assistance.

PTACs come in many different sizes and shapes, reflecting the needs, priorities and resources of the areas they serve. Some PTACs are administered directly by state governments, while others partner with universities, community colleges, local economic development corporations or other local institutions. Some PTACs operate within Bureau of Indian Affairs areas exclusively serving Native American owned businesses.

Many are affiliated in some way with Small Business Development Centers and other small business programs. All PTACs are staffed with counselors experienced in government contracting and provide a wide range of services including classes and seminars, individual counseling and easy access to bid opportunities, contract specifications, procurement histories, and other information necessary to successfully compete for government contracts.

To access the 93 Procurement Technical Assistance Centers (PTACs), which form a nationwide network of procurement professionals, see: *http://www.aptac-us.org/new/index.php* and *http://www.dla.mil/db/procurem.htm.*

In summary, PCRs, CMRs, and PTACs stand ready to provide business development assistance that helps small firms compete for government contracts. 8(a)BD firms that seek to increase their competitiveness should contact them to see what they can do to help them.

A list of PCRs, CMRs, COCs, and Size Specialists is presented at the end of this chapter.

Chapter Three imparts *Gems of Wisdom* of members of the acquisition facilitation team.

Directory of PCRs, CMRs, COC, and Size Specialists

AREA I: Includes the states of Connecticut, Maine, Massachusetts, New Hampshire, New Jersey, New York, Rhode Island and Vermont and the Commonwealth of Puerto Rico and the Virgin Islands

AREA DIRECTOR: JANETTE FASANO
Office of Government Contracting, U.S. Small Business Administration
10 Causeway Street, Room 416,
Boston, MA 02222-1093
Tel: (617) 565-5622   Fax: (617) 565- 8186
e-mail: janette.fasano@sba.gov

MAINE, NEW HAMPSHIRE, RHODE ISLAND, CONNECTICUT, VERMONT AND MASSACHUSETTS

SEAN F. CREAN (PCR & CMR)
SBA Procurement Center Representative
Maine District Office
U.S. Small Business Administration
68 Sewall Street, Room 512, Augusta, ME 04330
Tel: (207) 622-8379   Fax: (202) 481-5513
e-mail: sean.crean@sba.gov

ACTIVITIES COVERED
- Air Force Electronic Systems Ctr, Hanscom AFB
- VA Healthcare Systems -, ME, , VT, , NH
- Naval Undersea Warfare Center–Newport, RI
- Portsmouth Naval Shipyard–Portsmouth, NH
- U.S. Army Corps of Engineers–Concord, MA
- U.S. Army Soldier Systems Center–Natick, MA
- Army National Guard – ME
- Air National Guard –, ME, NH

DIANNE L. NOLAN (COC ASSISTANT)
Office of Government Contracting
U.S. Small Business Administration
10 Causeway Street, Room 416,
Boston, MA 02222-1093
Tel: (617) 565-5570
e-mail: dianne.nolan@sba.gov

ARVIND PATEL (CMR)
Small Business Administration
275 Randolph Rd. – Bldg. 1101, Hanscom AFB, MA 01731-2818
Voice: (781) 377-2737 Fax (202) 481-0340
E-mail: arvind.patel@sba.gov

NEW JERSEY, PUERTO RICO & THE VIRGIN ISLANDS
MICHAEL CECERE (PCR)
SBA Representative
U.S. Army ARDEC - Bldg. 1610,
Picatinny Arsenal, NJ 07806-5000
Tel: (973) 724-6574   Fax: (973) 724-5704
e-mail: michael.cecere@us.army.mil

ACTIVITIES COVERED
- U.S. Army Research, Development and Engineering Command (RDECOM)
- Armament Research, Development & Engineering Center (ARDEC)–Picatinny Arsenal, NJ
- U.S. Army Joint Munitions and Lethality Life Cycle Management Command (JM& L LCMC) – Picatinny Arsenal, NJ

NEW JERSEY
LARRY HANSEN (PCR & CMR)
SBA Representative
U.S. Army Communications - Electronics Command
ATTN: SBA-PCR – Bldg. 1208,
Fort Monmouth, NJ 07703-5000
Tel: (732) 532-3419   Fax: (732) 532-8732
e-mail: larry.hansen@sba.gov

ACTIVITIES COVERED
- McGuire AFB – Wrightstown, NJ
- Naval Air Warfare Center – Lakehurst, NJ
- U.S. Army Communication & Electronics – Command–Fort Monmouth, NJ
- U.S. Army at Fort Dix–Fort Dix, NJ

ANDREW ZUBER (CMR)
US Army RDECOM-ARDEC
ATTN: SBA, Bldg. #1610, Picatinny Arsenal, NJ 07806-5000
Voice: (973) 724-6960 Fax: (202) 481-0225
E-mail: andrew.zuber@sba.gov

NEW YORK
MALINDA CHEN (CMR, COC SPECIALIST, AND SIZE SPECIALIST)
SBA/Melville District Office
35 Pinelawn Road, Suite 207W, Melville, NY 11747
Voice: (631) 454-0750 x 212
Fax: (202) 481-4286
E-mail: malinda.chen@sba.gov

DEBRA B. LIBOW (PCR)
SBA Procurement Representative
U.S. Army Corps of Engineers
26 Federal Plaza, Room 21-130,

New York, NY 10278
Tel: (212) 264-4395   Fax: (202) 481-1581
e-mail: debra.libow@sba.gov

ACTIVITIES COVERED
- DVA, VISN #3 Medical Centers (NY & NJ) – Bronx, NY
- GSA, Federal Supply Ser. – New York, NY
- GSA, Public Buildings Service – New York, NY
- U.S. Army Corps of Engineers–New York, NY
- U.S. Military Academy–West Point, NY

SANDY LIU (CMR, COC SPECIALIST, AND SIZE SPECIALIST)
SBA/Melville District Office
35 Pinelawn Road, Suite 207W, Melville, NY 11747
Voice: (631) 454-0750 x 215
Fax (202) 481-5490
E-mail: sandy.liu@sba.gov

JOYCE SPEARS (PCR & CMR)
Rochester Branch Office
U.S. Small Business Administration
100 State Street, Suite 410, Rochester, NY 14614
Tel: (585) 263-6700   Fax: (585) 263-3146
e-mail: joyce.spears@sba.gov

ACTIVITIES COVERED
- U.S. Air Force Material Command, AFRL Rome – Research Site, Rome, NY
- U.S. Army Corps of Engineers – Buffalo, NY
- U.S. Army Contracting Agency Northern – Region, Dir. of Contracting Fort Drum, NY
- U.S. Army Material Command – Watervliet Arsenal, Watervliet, NY
- National Guard Bureau
- United States Property and Fiscal Office for New York, Latham, NY

PAUL C. TARAVELLA (CMR, COC SPECIALIST, & SIZE SPECIALIST)
SBA/Melville District Office
35 Pinelawn Road, Suite 207W, Melville, NY 11747
Voice: (631) 454-0750 x 224   Fax: (202) 481-4864
E-mail: paul.taravella@sba.gov

AREA II: Includes the states of Delaware, Maryland, Pennsylvania, Virginia and West Virginia, and the Washington, DC Metropolitan Area.

AREA DIRECTOR: DAVID WM. LOINES
Office of Government Contracting
U.S. Small Business Administration
409 3rd Street, SW, Suite 8800,
Washington, DC 20416
(202) 205-7311 Fax (202) 205-7326
e-mail: david.loines@sba.gov

DEPUTY AREA DIRECTOR:
VINCENT ROBERT RICE
U.S. Small Business Administration
900 Market St., 5th Floor,
Philadelphia, PA 19107
Tel: (215) 580-2771   Fax (202) 481-5998
e-mail: vincent.rice@sba.gov

ROBERT F. COEN, PCR
U.S. Social Security Administration
7111 Security Boulevard, Baltimore, MD 21244
Tel: (410) 965-0300   F(202) 481-5256
e-mail: robert.coen@sba.gov

PENNSYLVANIA & MARYLAND
VINCENT ROBERT RICE (SUPERVISORY PCR, SIZE SPECIALIST & CMR)
U.S. Small Business Administration
900 Market St., 5th Floor,
Philadelphia, PA 19107
Tel: (215) 580-2771   Fax (202) 481-5998
e-mail: vincent.rice@sba.gov

ACTIVITIES COVERED
- Army Chemical & Biol. Comm.–Edgewood, MD
- Army Garrison, Aberdeen Proving Gd– Aberdeen, MD
- Navy, Fleet Industrial Support Center Detachment–Philadelphia, PA
- Navy Surface Warfare Center–Bethesda, MD

VINCENT MAZZOTTA (SIZE PROGRAM MANAGER AND CMR)
Robert N.C. Nix Federal Building
900 Market Street, 5th Floor, Philadelphia, PA 19107
Voice: (215) 580-2809 Fax: (215) 580-2776
E-mail: vincent.mazzotta@sba.gov

ROBERT F. COEN, PCR
U.S. Social Security Administration
7111 Security Boulevard, Baltimore, MD 21244
Voice: (410) 965-0300

DEBORAH DIGGS (CMR)
U.S. Small Business Administration
Baltimore District Office
10 South Howard Street, Baltimore, MD 21201
Tel: (410) 962-6195 X353   Fax: (202) 481-1565
E-mail: deborah.diggs@sba.gov

PENNSYLVANIA
TERRY L. BUDGE (CMR & COC SPECIALIST)
Robert N.C. Nix Federal Building
900 Market Street, 5th Floor, Philadelphia, PA 19107
Voice: (215) 580-2770 Fax: (215) 580-2776
E-mail: terry.budge@sba.gov

CAROL S. DECKER (PCR)
SBA Representative
Naval Inventory Control Point
Code 0062, Bldg. 410, 5450 Carlisle Pike
Mechanicsburg, PA 17055-0788

Tel: (717)605-7525 DSN 430-7525
Fax: (717) 605-4858
e-mail: Carol.Decker@Navy.Mil

ACTIVITIES COVERED
- Navy Inventory Control Point–Mechanicsburg, PA
- Navy Inventory Control Point-Philadelphia, PA
- Defense Distribution Center-New Cumberland, PA

RICARDO J. SACIDOR (PCR)
SBA Representative
Defense Supply Center Philadelphia
700 Robbins Avenue, Philadelphia, PA 19111-5098
Tel: (215)737-5912 DSN 444-5912
Fax: (215) 737-7116
e-mail: Ricardo.Sacidor@dla.mil
 or Ricardo.Sacidor@sba.gov

ACTIVITIES COVERED
- Corps of Engineers–Philadelphia, PA
- Defense Supply Center Philadelphia–Philadelphia, PA
- General Services Administration–Philadelphia, PA

VIRGINIA
JUDY SAYERS (PCR)
SBA Representative
Defense Logistics Agency
8000 Jefferson Davis Highway,
Richmond, VA 23297-5124
Tel: (804)279-3690   Fax: (804) 279-6615
e-mail: judy.sayers@dla.mil

ACTIVITIES COVERED
- Defense Supply Center Richmond–Richmond, VA

OCTAVIA TURNER (PCR)
SBA Representative
NASA Langley Research Center
Bldg. 1209, Rm. 100, MS446,
Hampton, VA 23681-2199
Tel: (757) 864-6859   Fax: (757) 864-8096
e-mail: octavia.turner@nasa.gov

ACTIVITIES COVERED
- Army Corps of Engineers–Norfolk, VA
- Army Northern Region Contracting Command – Ft. Eustis, VA
- Fleet and Industrial Supply Center–Norfolk, VA
- NASA, Langley Research Center–Hampton, VA
- NAVFAC Atlantic Division–Norfolk, VA

WEST VIRGINIA
BARBARA WEAVER (PCR & CMR)
SBA Representative
P.O. Box 880, Mail Stop L02,
Morgantown, WV 26505
Tel: (304) 623-5631 x226   Fax: (202) 481-2799
email: barbara.weaver@sba.gov

ACTIVITIES COVERED
- DOE, National Energy Technology Centers: Morgantown, WV & Pittsburgh, PA
- DOD, Army Corps of Engineers – Huntington, WV and Pittsburgh, PA
- DOJ, FBI Criminal Justice Information Service – Clarksburg, WA

WASHINGTON, DC METROPOLITAN AREA

RHONDA ANDERSON (SUPERVISORY PCR)
SBA Representative
General Services Administration
Federal Supply Service
Crystal Plaza 4 - Room 8001
2200 Crystal Drive, Arlington, VA 20406
Tel: (703) 605-1801 Fax: (703) 605-9961
e-mail: rhonda.anderson@gsa.gov

ACTIVITIES COVERED
- General Services Administration, Hq - Washington, DC
- Federal Supply Service - Arlington, VA
- Federal Technology Service - Fairfax, VA
- National Furniture Center - Arlington, VA
- Automotive Division - Arlington, VA

BERNARD DURHAM (PCR)
SBA Representative
National Aeronautics and Space Admin.
Goddard Space Flight Center
Building 8, Code 210, Greenbelt, MD 20771
Tel: (301) 286-4378 Fax: (202) 481-0427
e-mail: bernard.durham2@sba.gov or
bernard.durham2@dhs.gov

ACTIVITIES COVERED
- NASA, Goddard SFC–Greenbelt, MD
- NASA Headquarters–Washington, DC
- U.S. Army RDECOM Acquisition Center - Adelphi, MD
- Department of Homeland Security - Washington, DC
- GSA/Regional Office - Washington, DC
- Department of Energy - Washington, DC
- Department of Housing & Urban Dev. - Washington, DC

A. P. (MITCH) OCAMPO (PCR)
SBA Representative
Naval Sea Systems Command Code O2K/SBA
1333 Isaac Hull Ave., SE
Room 5W-2630
Washington Navy Yard, Washington, DC 20376-2090
Tel: (202) 781-3966 Fax: (202) 781-4772
e-mail: ocampomp@navsea.navy.mil

ACTIVITIES COVERED
- Defense Information Systems Agency–Arlington, VA
- Defense Energy Support Center–Fort Belvoir, VA

- Naval Sea Systems Command–Washington, DC
- NAVFAC, Chesapeake Div.–Washington, DC
- NAVFAC Headquarters–Washington, DC
- Department of the Treasury - Washington, DC

ANNETTE JOHNSON-MERRION (PCR)
SBA Representative
U.S. Department of Transportation, S42
400 7th Street, SW, Room 9410,
Washington, DC 20590
Tel: (202) 366-9142 Fax: (202) 366-7228
e-mail: annette.merrion@dot.gov

ACTIVITIES COVERED
- Department of Transportation - Washington, DC
- Department of Veteran Affairs - Washington, DC
- Environmental Protection Agency - Washington, DC
- Department of Justice - Washington, DC
- Department of Housing & Urban Dev. (HUD) - Washington, DC
- Department of Education
- Small Business Administration - Washington, DC

MALDA BROWN (PCR)
SBA Representative
6100 Executive Boulevard
Room 6D05-MSC 7540, Bethesda, MD 20892-7540,
Tel: (301) 496-8023 Fax: (301) 480-2506
e-mail: malda.brown@hhs.gov

ACTIVITIES COVERED
- Army Corps of Engineers–Baltimore, MD
- Department of Health & Human Ser.– Washington, DC
- Social Security Administration–Baltimore, MD
- Department of Commerce - Washington, DC

MARJORIE WILKINS (PCR)
SBA Representative
Naval Air Command
21983 Bundy Road, Unit #7 Bldg. #441, Patuxent River, MD 20670-1127
Tel: (301) 757-9085 Fax:(301)757-9093
Email: majorie.wilkins@navy.mil

ACTIVITIES COVERED
- Naval Air Systems Command - Patuxent River, MD
- Naval Air Warfare Center Craft Division - Patuxent River, MD
- Navy Surface Warfare Center - Indian Head, MD
- Department of Labor - Washington, DC

PETER ZAHIRIEH (PCR)
U.S. Department of Agriculture
1400 Independence Ave., SW
AG Stop 9501, Room 1566, South Bldg.,

Washington, DC 20250-9501
Tel: (202) 720-7117 Fax: (202) 720-3001
e-mail: shahrokh.zahirieh@usda.gov

ACTIVITIES COVERED
- Defense Contracting Command–Washington, DC
- Department of Agriculture - Washington, DC
- Department of State - Washington, DC

AREA III: Includes the states of Alabama, Florida, Georgia, Kentucky, Mississippi, North Carolina, South Carolina and Tennessee

AREA DIRECTOR: MITCHELL MORAND
Office of Government Contracting
U.S. Small Business Administration
233 Peachtree St., NE, Suite 1805,
Atlanta, GA 30303
Tel: (404) 331-7587 Fax: (404) 331-2956
email: mitchell.morand@sba.gov

DEPUTY AREA DIRECTOR: MARY E. HARRIS
Office of Government Contracting
U.S. Small Business Administration
233 Peachtree St., NE, Suite 1805,
Atlanta, GA 30303
Tel: (404) 331-7587 Fax: (404) 331-2956
email: mary.harris@sba.gov

ALABAMA
GARY W. HEARD (ENGINEERING/PCR)
U.S. Small Business Administration
Bldg. 5303, Room 3135,
Redstone Arsenal, AL 35898-5150
Tel: (256) 842-6240 Fax: (256) 842-0091
e-mail: gary.heard@sba.gov

ACTIVITIES COVERED
- Army Aviation & Missile Command–Huntsville, AL
- Army Engineering & Support Center-Huntsville, AL
- Maxwell AFB-Montgomery, AL
- HQ SSG, Gunter Annex-Maxwell AFB, AL

BARBARA J. JENKINS (PCR)
NASA, Marshall Space Flight Center
Mail Drop PS01, Attn: SBA, PCR
Bldg. 4202, Room 219 B, Marshall Space Flight Center, AL 35812
Tel: (256) 544-5012 Fax: (256) 544-8221
e-mail: barbara.jenkins@msfc.nasa.gov

ACTIVITIES COVERED
- Anniston Army Depot–Anniston, AL
- Fort McClellan–Anniston, AL
- Fort Rucker–Daleville, AL
- NASA, Marshall Space Flight Ctr.–Huntsville, AL
- Space & Missile Defense Command–Huntsville, AL

- Corps of Engineers- Memphis, TN
- Naval Support Activity Mid-South-Millington, TN

FLORIDA
Vacant
SBA Representative
South Florida District Office
100 S. Biscayne Blvd., 7th Fl., Miami, FL 33131

ACTIVITES COVERED
- U.S. Department of Veterans Affairs – Bay Pines, FL
- U.S. Department of Veterans Affairs, Miami, FL
- U.S. Department of State, Ft. Lauderdale, FL
- U.S.Army Southern Command-Miami, FL
- Homeland Security, U.S. Coast Guard, Miami, FL
- U.S. Dept, Air Force –Homestead ARB, FL

WALTER R. WALLACE (PCR)
SBA Representative
Naval Air Warfare Center
Training Systems Division, 12350 Research Blvd.
Orlando, FL 32826-3224
Tel: (407) 380-8252 Fax: (407) 380-8232
e-mail: walter.wallace@sba.gov

ACTIVITIES COVERED
- McDill AFB–Tampa, FL
- U.S. Special Operations Command, McDill AFB-Tampa, FL
- NASA, Kennedy Space Center.–FL
- NAVAIR Orlando–Orlando, FL
- Patrick AFB–Cocoa Beach, FL
- Army Corps of Engineers–Jacksonville, FL
- Army Corps of Engineers –Mobile, AL
- Eglin AFB, Florida
- Hurlburt AFB, FL
- Navy, FISC–Jacksonville, FL
- Naval Facilities Engr. Cmd. Southeast-Jacksonville, FL
- Naval Submarine Base-Kings Bay, GA
- Navy Surface Warfare Center–Panama City, FL
- Tyndall AFB Panama City, FL
- Naval Facilities Engineering Cmd. ROICC-Jacksonville, FL

GEORGIA
T. C. HOLLINGSWORTH (PCR & SUPERVISOR)
P. O. Box 611
Warner Robins, GA 31099-0611
Tel: (478) 926-7446 Fax: (478) 926-3832
e-mail: thomas.hollingsworth@robins.af.mil

ACTIVITIES COVERED
- Marine Corps Logistics Command–Albany, GA
- Warner Robins ALC–Warner Robins, GA

MARY ANN KORRE (CMR)
233 Peachtree St., NE, Suite 1805, Atlanta, GA 30303
Voice: (404) 331-7587, Ext. 206

Fax: (404) 331-2956
E-mail: mary.korre@sba.gov

ANNA PENDER (PCR)
P.O. Box 611
Warner Robins, GA 31099-0611
Tel: (478) 926-5874 Fax: (478) 926-3832
e-mail: anna.pender@robins.af.mil

ACTIVITIES COVERED
- Fort Benning–Columbus, GA
- Fort Gordon–Augusta, GA
- Moody AFB–Valdosta, GA
- Warner Robins ALC–Warner Robins, GA

JOYCE THURMOND (PCR)
U.S. Small Business Administration
Government Contracting
233 Peachtree Street, NE - Suite 1805,
Atlanta, GA 30303
Tel: (404) 331-7587 x205 Fax: (404) 331-2956
e-mail: joyce.thurmond@sba.gov

ACTIVITIES COVERED
- Atlanta Army Contracting Center–Atlanta, GA
- GSA, Region IV–Atlanta, GA
- HHS, Center for Disease Control–Atlanta, GA
- VAMC–Decatur, GA

KENTUCKY & TENNESSEE
VACANT
U.S. Small Business Administration
c/o U. S. Army Corps of Engineers
PO Box 59, Room 760, Louisville, KY 40201-0059
Tele: (502) 582-5552 Fax:(502) 582-5547

*Activities currently covered by Ivette Mesa Bascumbe
Tel: (404) 331-7587, x209

Email: ivette.bascumbe.mesa@sba.gov

ACTIVITES COVERED
- Fort Campbell- Fort Campbell, KY
- Fort Knox-Fort Knox, KY
- U.S. Corps of Engineers-Louisville, KY
- U.S. Army Corps of Engineers-Nashville, TN
- Department of Energy-Oak Ridge, TN

MISSISSIPPI
IVETTE MESA BASCUMBE (PCR, SIZE SPECIALIST & COC SPECIALIST)
U.S. Small Business Administration
Government Contracting
233 Peachtree Street, NE – Suite 1805, Atlanta, GA 30303
Tele: (404) 331-7587 x 209 Fax: (202) 481-2273
Email: ivette.bascumbe.mesa@sba.gov

ACTIVITIES COVERED
- U.S. Army Corps of Engineers, Vicksburg, MS
- Army Engineering Research Development Center – Vicksburg, MS
- Kessler AFB-Biloxi, MS

NORTH CAROLINA
LARRY W. MALLORY (PCR)
SBA Representative
C/O NIEHS Contracting Office
P.O. Box 12874, Research Triangle Park, NC 27709
Tel: (919) 541-7895 Fax: (919) 541-2712
e-mail: mallory1@niehs.nih.gov

ACTIVITIES COVERED
- Army Corps of Engineers–Wilmington, NC
- DHHS, Nat. Institute of Environmental Health Sciences-RTP, NC
- Ft. Bragg–Fayetteville, NC
- U.S. Army Research Office-Research Triangle Park, NC
- Pope AFB–Fayetteville, NC
- Seymour Johnson AFB–Goldsboro, NC
- Environmental Protection Agency-RTP, NC
- MCB Camp Lejeune-Jacksonville, NC

SOUTH CAROLINA
VACANT
Charleston AFB, SC
Activities are currently being covered by Joyce Thurmond
Tel: (404) 331-7587   Fax (404) 331-7587
e-mail: joyce.thurmond@sba.gov

ACTIVITIES COVERED
- Army Corps of Engineers–Charleston, SC
- Army Corps of Engineers–Savannah, GA
- Charleston AFB–Charleston, SC
- Fort Jackson–Columbia, SC
- Fort Stewart–Hinesville, GA
- Naval Facilities Engineering Command–Charleston, SC
- Space and Naval Warfare Systems Center–Charleston, SC
- Department of Energy, Savannah River Site-Aiken, SC

AREA IV: Includes the states of Illinois, Indiana, Iowa, Kansas, Michigan, Minnesota, Missouri, Nebraska, North Dakota, Ohio, South Dakota and Wisconsin

AREA DIRECTOR
ROBERT MURPHY
Office of Government Contracting
U.S. Small Business Administration
500 West Madison St., Suite 1240, Chicago, IL 60661-2511
Tel: (312) 353-7381 Fax: (202) 481-5288
e-mail: robert.murphy@sba.gov

DEPUTY AREA DIRECTOR
ROBERT L. ZELENIK
Office of Government Contracting
U.S. Small Business Administration
500 West Madison St., Suite 1240, Chicago, IL 60661-2511
Tel: (312) 353-7373 Fax: (202) 481-5280
e-mail: robert.zelenik@sba.gov

ILLINOIS
JACK BOCCAROSSA (SUPERVISORY PCR)
U. S. Small Business Administration
Field Support Command
ATTN: SBALO
Bldg. 61, 2nd Floor, Rock Island, IL 61299-7180
Tel: (309) 782-6350 Fax: (309) 782-4214
e-mail: jack.boccarossa@conus.army.mil

ACTIVITIES COVERED
- Joint Munitions Command TACOM–Rock Island, IL

PAMELA COLEMAN (PCR & COC SPECIALIST)
SBA Representative
U.S. Small Business Administration
Office of Government Contracting
500 W. Madison Street – Suite 1240, Chicago, IL 60661-2511
Tel: (312) 353-7442 Fax: (202) 481-4777
e-mail: pamela.coleman@sba.gov

ACTIVITIES COVERED
- General Services Administration–Chicago, IL
- Great Lakes Naval Train Stat-Great Lakes, IL
- Veterans Affairs National Acquisition Center,Hines, IL
- U.S. DOE - Argonne National Lab.–Argonne, IL
- VA, VISN 12, Great Lakes-Milwaukee, WI
- Corps of Engineers-Chicago, IL

DAVID GORDON
(SIZE PROGRAM MANAGER & COC COORDINATOR)
Office of Government Contracting
U.S. Small Business Administration
500 West Madison St., Suite 1240,
Chicago, IL 60661-2511
Tel: (312) 353-7674 Fax: (202) 481-1842
e-:mail: david.gordon@sba.gov

MICHAEL KOWALESIK (CMR & COC SPECIALIST)
Office of Government Contracting
US Small Business Administration
500 W. Madison Street - Ste. 1240,
Chicago, IL 60661-2511
Voice: (312) 353-4504 Fax: (202) 481-4563
E-mail: michael.kowalesik@sba.gov

INDIANA & OHIO
LYNDA PARRETT (CMR & COC SPECIALIST)

8500 Keystone Crossing, Suite 400, Indianapolis, IN 46402
Voice: (317) 226-7274 Fax (317) 226-7587
e--mail: lynda.parrett@sba.gov

OHIO
EUGENE DROMBETTA (PCR)
Small Business Administration
c/o Defense Supply Center Columbus
ATTN SBA-PCR, Gene Drombetta
P.O. Box 3990, Columbus, OH 43218-3990
Tel: (614) 692-2669 Fax: (614) 692-2388
e-mail: eugene.drombetta@dla.mil

ACTIVITIES COVERED
- Defense Supply Center Columbus–Columbus, OH

THOMAS KRUSEMARK (PCR)
SBA Representative SBA-PCR
2196 D Street, Building 39, Wright-Patterson AFB, OH 44533-7201
Tel: (937) 255-3333   Fax: (202) 481-6522
e-mail: thomas.krusemark@sba.gov

ACTIVITIES COVERED
- Wright Patterson AFB–Dayton, OH
- EPA, Cincinnati, OH
- Department of Energy-Cincinnati, OH

DAVID PATTEE (PCR)
Small Business Administration
c/o Defense Supply Center Columbus
ATTN: SBA-PCR, David Pattee
P.O. Box 3990, Columbus, OH 4321 8-3990
Tel: (614) 692-0718 Fax: (614) 692-2388
e-mail: dave.pattee@dla.mil

ACTIVITIES COVERED
- Defense Supply Center Columbus–Columbus, OH
- NASA –Glenn Research Center–Cleveland, OH

MICHIGAN
JOSEPH W. PECK (PCR)
SBA Representative
U.S. Army Tank Automotive and Armaments Command
Bldg. 231, Room E 1332, Warren, MI 48397-5000
Tel: (586) 574-8124   Fax (586) 574-5560
e-mail: peckj@tacom.army.mil

ACTIVITIES COVERED
- Army Tank Automotive & Armaments Command-Warren, MI

PAMELA THOMPSON (PCR)
SBA Representative
U. S. Army Tank Automotive and Armaments Command

ATTN: SBA PCR
Bldg. 231, Room E 1332, Warren, MI 48397-5000
Tel: (586) 574-8124 Fax: (586) 574-5560
e-mail: thompsop@tacom.army.mil

ACTIVITIES COVERED
- Army Tank Automotive & Armaments Command– Warren, MI
- Defense Reutilization and Marketing Services-Battle Creek, MI

ILLINOIS & MISSOURI
MERRY BAYER (PCR)
SBA Representative
SBA St. Louis District Office
200 N. Broadway, Suite 1500, St. Louis, MO 63102
Tel: (314) 539-6600 x236   Fax (202) 481-6445
e-mail: merry.bayer@sba.gov

ACTIVITIES COVERED
- AMC Contracting (HQ/A7K CONF)–Scott AFB, IL
- AMC Command Contracting Office (HQ AMC/ A7k(Contracting Squadron (375 AW/LGC) –Scott AFB, IL
- Defense Information Technology Contracting Org. (DITCO)-Scott AFB, IL
- US Transportation Command-Scott AFB,IL
- United States Property and Fiscal Office-Springfield, IL
- US Army Corps of Engineers-St. Louis, MO
- National Geospatial Intelligence Agency (NGA)-St. Louis, MO
- US Department of Agriculture (USDA)-Columbia, MO
- FedSource (Dept. of Treasury)-St. Louis, MO
- DVA, VA Hospital-Jefferson Barracks, St. Louis, MO

KANSAS & MISSOURI
DAVID TURNER (PCR, CMR & COC SPECIALIST)
U.S. Small Business Administration
Procurement Center Representative
U.S. General Services Administration
Room #1161 Office Symbol 6ADB
1500 East Bannister Rd.
Kansas City, MO - 64131-1799
Tel: (816) - 823-1722 Fax: (202) 481-1501
e-mail: david.turner@sba.gov

ACTIVITIES COVERED
- Corps of Engineers-Kansas City, MO
- USDA Commodities Office-Kansas City, MO
- Whiteman AFB-Knobnoster, MO
- Fort Leonard Wood, MO
- General Services Administration-Heartland Region, Kansas City, MO
- McConnell AFB-Wichita, KS
- Dept. of Veterans Affairs, Heartland Network-Leavenworth, KS
- Fort Leavenworth-Leavenworth, KS
- Fort Riley-Junction City, KS

NEBRASKA, IOWA, AND NORTH AND SOUTH DAKOTA
DWIGHT JOHNSON (PCR)
SBA Nebraska District Office
11145 Mill Valley Road
Omaha, NE 68154-3949
Tel: (402) 221-7206 Fax: (202) 481-1770
e-mail: dwight.johnson@sba.gov

ACTIVITIES COVERED
- Army Corps of Engineers–Omaha, NE
- Offutt AFB–NE
- National Park Service, Regional Office - NE
- Dept. of Veterans Affairs Medical Center–Omaha, NE
- Dept of Veterans Affairs Medical Center–Lincoln, NE
- United States Property and Fiscal Office-Lincoln, NE
- Dept. of Veterans Affairs Medical Center-Iowa City, IA
- United States Property and Fiscal Office-Des Moines, IA
- Bureau of Indian Affairs – Aberdeen, SD
- Ellis, AFB, Rapid City, SD
- Grand Forks AFB, Grand Forks, ND
- Minot AFB-Minot, ND

AREA V: Includes the states of Arkansas, Colorado, Louisiana, New Mexico, Oklahoma and Texas.

AREA DIRECTOR
ROBERT C. TAYLOR
Office of Government Contracting
Small Business Administration
409 Third Street, SW, Suite 8800
Washington, DC 20416
Tele: (202) 205- 7419 Fax: (202) 481-5247
email: robert.c.taylor@sba.gov

ACTING DEPUTY AREA DIRECTOR
STEPHANIE LEWIS
SBA/GC Ste 116
4300 Amon Carter Blvd
Fort Worth, TX 76115
Voice: (817) 684-5305 Fax (817) 684-5310
E-mail: stephanie.lewis@sba.gov

COLORADO
THOMAS A. CLARKE (ACTING NATIONAL PROGRAM MANAGER , NATURAL RESOURCES & SALES ASSISTANCE)
Denver Natural Resources Sales Assistance Office
721 19th St., Room 426,
Denver, CO 80202-2517
Tel: (303) 844-2607 x266 Fax (202) 481-5826
e-mail: thomas.clarke@sba.gov

ACTIVITIES COVERED
- Forest Service: Region 2 (CO, WY-except NW, SD, & NE); Region 3 (AZ & NM); Region 9 (IL, IN, MA, MI, MN, MO, NH, NY, OH, PA, VT, WV, & WI).
- (Acting) Region 8 (AL,AR, FL, GA, KY, LA, MS, NC, SC, TN,TX, & VA).
- Royalty Oil, Natural Gas, & Coal-MMS, BLM, & DOE-entire US.
- Sale of Excess Federal Property-GSA & DOD

KAREN KLAM (CMR & SIZE SPECIALIST)
SBA/GC
721 19th St. Suite 426
Denver, CO 80202-2517
Voice: (303) 844-2607 x271
 Fax: (303) 844-0514
E-mail: karen.klam@sba.gov

JOSE MARTINEZ (PCR)
SBA Representative
721 19th Street, Suite 426
Denver, CO 80202-2517
Tel: (303) 844-2607 x264
Fax: (303) 844-0514
e-mail: jose.martinez@sba.gov

ACTIVITIES COVERED
- Bureau of Land Management–Denver, CO
- Bureau of Reclamation–Denver, CO
- Department of Commerce–Boulder, CO
- DOE, Western Power Admin.–Golden, CO
- DOT, FHWY–Lakewood, CO
- Fort Carson–Colorado Springs, CO
- GSA–Denver, CO
- National Park Service–Denver, CO
- Peterson AFB–Colorado Springs, CO
- Schriever AFB–Colorado Springs, CO
- USAF Academy–Colorado Springs, CO
- U.S. Geological Survey–Denver, CO
- Army Space Missile Defense Command-Colorado Springs, CO
- Buckley AFB, Aurora, CO
- Minerals Management, DOL, Denver, CO
- U.S. Fish & Wildlife, DOL, Denver, CO

LOUISIANA
RANDY MARCHIAFAVA (PCR & CMR)
SBA Representative
U.S. Army Corps of Engineers
7400 Leake Ave, Room 161
P.O. Box 60267
New Orleans, LA 70160-2067
Tel: (504) 862-2992
Fax: (202) 292-3738
e-mail: randy.j.marchiafava@mvn02.usace.army.mil

ACTIVITIES COVERED
- Army Corps of Engineers–New Orleans, LA
- Army Joint Readiness Training Ctr.–Fort Polk, LA
- Barksdale AFB–Shreveport, LA

NEW MEXICO & EL PASO, TEXAS
TRINNIE BRIDGE (PCR AND CMR)
SBA Procurement Center Representative
U.S. Army Corps of Engineers
4101 Jefferson Plaza, NE
Albuquerque, NM 8710 9
Tel: (505) 342-3252
Fax: (505) 346-2883
e-mail: trinnie.bridge@sba.gov

ACTIVITIES COVERED
- Canon AFB–Clovis, NM
- Corps of Engineers–Albuquerque, NM
- Department of Energy Albuquerque, NM
- Air Force Operational Test and Evaluation (AFOTEC) Albuquerque, NM
- DVA Hospital–Albuquerque, NM
- Ft. Bliss–El Paso, TX
- Holloman AFB–Alamogordo, NM
- USAF, Phillips Laboratory–Albuquerque, NM
- White Sands Missile Range–White Sands, NM
- State of New Mexico

OKLAHOMA
TERESA "TERRI" SHOOK (PCR & CMR)
SBA Representative
Oklahoma District Office
301 NW 6th Street, Suite 116
Oklahoma City, OK 73102
Tel: (405) 609-8026
Fax: (405) 609-8990
e-mail: teresa.shook@sba.gov

ACTIVITIES COVERED
- Army Corps of Engineers–Tulsa, OK
- DVA Medical Center–Oklahoma City, OK
- Ft. Sill–Lawton, OK
- Oklahoma City Air Logistics Ctr.–Oklahoma City, OK

NORTH TEXAS
STEPHANIE LEWIS
(CMR & SIZE PROGRAM MANAGER)
SBA/GC Ste 116
4300 Amon Carter Blvd
Fort Worth, TX 76115
Voice: (817) 684-5305
Fax: (817) 684-5310
E-mail: stephanie.lewis@sba.gov

LARRY LYTLE (COC SPECIALIST & CMR)
SBA/GC Suite 116
4300 Amon Carter Blvd.
Fort Worth, TX 76155
Voice: (817) 684-5306 Fax: (817) 684-5310
E-mail: larry.lytle@sba.gov

NORTH TEXAS & ARKANSAS
PAUL STONE (PCR)
Procurement Center Representative
U.S. Small Business Administration
c/o U. S. Army Corps of Engineers,

PO Box 17300
Fort Worth, TX 76102
Tel: (817) 886-1024
Fax: (817) 886-6407
e-mail: paul.p.stone@swf02.usace.army.mil

ACTIVITIES COVERED
- Corps of Engineers Fort Worth, TX
- Dyess AFB–Abilene, TX
- Fort Hood–Killeen, TX
- GSA–Fort Worth, TX
- Sheppard AFB–Wichita Falls, TX
- VA Medical Center–Dallas, TX
- Corps of Engineers–Little Rock, AR
- DVA Medical Center–Little Rock, AR
- Little Rock AFB–Jacksonville, AR
- Pine Bluff Arsenal–Pine Bluff, AR
- Red River Army Depot–Texarkana, TX

SOUTH TEXAS
VALERIE COLEMAN (PCR & CMR)
SBA Procurement Center Representative
NASA
2101 NASA Parkway, Mail Code: BD 35
Houston, TX 77058
Tel: (281) 483-1549   Fax: (281) 483-4326
e-mail: valerie.j.coleman@nasa.gov

ACTIVITIES COVERED
- Air Intelligence Agency–San Antonio, TX
- Brooks City-Base–San Antonio, TX
- Fort Sam Houston–San Antonio, TX
- Lackland AFB–San Antonio, TX
- Randolph AFB–San Antonio, TX
- Army Corps of Engineers Galveston, TX
- Dept of Veterans Affairs-Houston, TX.
- John Space Center- Houston, TX
- San Antonio, TX*
- South TX*

*Activities are temporarily covered by Valerie Coleman

AREA VI: Include the states of Alaska, Arizona, California, Hawaii, Idaho, Montana, Nevada, Oregon, Utah, Washington, Wyoming and Guam

AREA DIRECTOR
JAMES GAMBARDELLA (ACTING AREA DIRECTOR)
Office of Government Contracting
U.S. Small Business Administration
455 Market Street, Suite 600
San Francisco, CA 94105-2420
Tel: (415) 744-8429
Fax: (415) 744-0314
e-mail: robert.paccione@sba.gov

AREA SUPERVISOR
NICHOLAS MANALISAY
U.S. Small Business Administration

330 North Brand Blvd., Suite 1200
Glendale, CA 91203-2304
Tel: (818) 552-3294
Fax: (818) 552-3221
e-mail: nicholas.manalisay@sba.gov

ALASKA
VACANT
SBA Procurement Center Representative
U.S. Small Business Administration
510 L Street, Suite 310
Anchorage, AK 99501

ACTIVITIES COVERED
- Army Corps of Engineers–Anchorage, AK
- Department of Transportation–Coast Guard – Juneau, AK
- Eielson AFB–Fairbanks, AK
- Elmendorf AFB–Anchorage, AK
- Ft. Richardson–Anchorage, AK

ARIZONA
TRACEY S. BROWN
(PCR, CMR, COC SPECIALIST & SIZE SPECIALIST)
SBA Procurement Center Representative
U.S. Small Business Administration
2828 North Central Ave, Suite 800, Phoenix, AZ 85004-1093
Tel: (602) 745-7217   Fax: (602) 745-7210
e-mail: tracey.brown@sba.gov

ACTIVITIES COVERED
- Davis Monthan AFB–Tucson, AZ
- Department of the Interior–Bureau of Reclamation-Phoenix,AZ
- Fort Huachuca–Sierra Vista, AZ
- Luke AFB–Glendale, AZ
- Yuma Proving Ground–Yuma, AZ

CALIFORNIA
CAROL BUNTS (SIZE PROGRAM MANAGER, CMR & COC SPECIALIST)
455 Market Street
San Francisco, CA 94105-2445
Voice: (415) 744-6844 Fax (415) 744-0314
E-mail: caroline.bunts@sba.gov

PAUL CHANN (PCR)
SBA Procurement Center Representative
U.S. Small Business Administration
455 Market St., Suite 600
San Francisco, CA 94105-2420
Tel: (415) 744-8481
Fax: (415) 744-0314
e-mail: paul.chann@sba.gov

ACTIVITIES COVERED
- Army Corps of Engineers–Sacramento, CA
- General Services Administration–San Francisco, CA
- NASA–Ames Research Center–Moffett Field, CA

LINDA COAKLEY (PCR, CMR, & COC SPECIALIST)
SBA Procurement Center Representative
SPAWAR Command (OOK)
4301 Pacific Highway
San Diego, CA 92110-3127
Tel: (619) 727-4868   Fax: (202) 481-4152
e-mail: linda.coakley@sba.gov

ACTIVITIES COVERED
- Fleet & Industrial Supply Center–San Diego, CA
- Marine Corp, Camp Pendleton–Oceanside, CA
- Naval Public Works Center–San Diego, CA
- NAVFAC – Southwest Division–San Diego CA
- SPAWAR Systems Center–San Diego, CA

Marina M. Laverdy (COC Referral Center)
U.S. Small Business Administration
330 N. Brand Blvd – room 1200
Glendale, California 91203
Tel:(818) 552-3306   Fax:818-552-3221

M. LEONARD MANZANARES (PCR, COC SPECIALIST, & CMR)
Los Angeles District Office
U.S. Small Business Administration
330 North Brand Blvd., Suite 1200
Glendale, CA 91203-2304
Tel: (818) 552-3296
Fax: (818) 552-3221
e-mail: m.manzanares@sba.gov

ACTIVITIES COVERED
- Army Corps of Engineers–Los Angeles, CA
- Edwards AFB–Edwards, CA
- Fleet & Industrial Supply Center Det.–Seal Beach, CA
- NASA, Dryden Space Research Center – Edwards, CA
- Naval Air Warfare Center–China Lake, CA
- Office in Charge of Construction–Seal Beach, CA
- Space & Missile Systems Center – Los Angeles, CA
- Vandenberg AFB–Lompoc, CA

HAWAII & GUAM
LAURENCE ORR (PCR)
Naval Facilities Engineering Command
258 Makalapa Drive, Ste. 100
Pearl Harbor, HI 96860-3134
Tel: (808) 474-7317 Fax: (808) 474-3387
e-mail: Laurence.orr@navy.mil

ACTIVITIES COVERED
- Army Corps of Engineers–Fort Shafter, HI
- Fleet Industrial Supply Center–Pearl Harbor, HI
- Hickam AFB–Honolulu, HI
- Naval Public Works Center–Pearl Harbor, HI
- NAVFAC–Pearl Harbor, HI
- U.S. Army Pacific & U. S. Army Garrison – Fort Shafter, HI

- Navy OICC (GUAM)
- Andersen AFB (GUAM)

OREGON AND MONTANA
JOHN BAGAASON (PCR, CMR, & SIZE
SPECIALIST)
Office of Government Contracting
U.S. Small Business Administration
1200 Sixth Avenue, Suite 1700
Seattle, WA 98101-1128
Tel: (206) 553-8546   Fax: (206) 553-6263
e-mail: john.bagaason@sba.gov

LINDA HAGEN (INDUSTRIAL SPECIALIST-
FORESTRY)
Office of Government Contracting
601 SW Second Avenue, Suite #950
Portland, OR 97204-3192
Tel: (503) 326-7245
Fax: (202) 481-4120
e-mail: Linda.Hagen@sba.gov

ACTIVITIES COVERED
- Army Corps of Engineers – Portland, OR
- USDA Forest Service - Portland, OR
- Department of Interior, Bureau of Reclamation – Billings, MT
- Malmstrom AFB – Great Falls, MT

NEVADA
VACANT
City Centre Place
400 South Fourth St., Ste 250
Las Vegas, NV 89101
Voice: (702) 388-6015   Fax (702) 388-6469

ACTIVITIES COVERED
- Department of the Interior, Bureau of Reclamation–Boulder City, NV
- DOE–Nevada Operations Div.–Las Vegas, NV
- Nellis AFB–Las Vegas, NV

UTAH
BRENT OWENS (PCR)
6038 Aspen Avenue, CE
Hill Air Force Base, UT 84056-5805
Tel: (801) 775-4141   Fax: (801) 777-5366
e-mail: Brent.Owens@HILL.af.mil

ACTIVITY COVERED
- Department of the Air Force Hill Air Force Base, Utah

WASHINGTON
WILLIAM BRAMWELL (INDUSTRIAL SPECIALIST-
FORESTRY)
2401 Fourth Avenue, Suit 400
Seattle, WA 98121-3419
Tel: (206) 553-8544 Fax (206) 481-6104
e-mail: william.bramwell@sba.gov

JAMES HUTCHINS (COC SPECIALIST, CMR, &
SIZE SPECIALIST)
2401 Fourth Avenue, Suite 400
Seattle, WA 98121-3419
Voice: (206) 553-6850   Fax (206) 553-6263
E-mail: james.hutchins@sba.gov

KEVIN MICHAEL (PCR, CMR, & COC SPECIALIST)
Office of Government Contracting
U.S. Small Business Administration
400 15th SW
Auburn, WA 98001-1128
Tel: (253) 931-7161   Fax: (253) 931-7743
e-mail: kevin.michael@sba.gov

ACTIVITIES COVERED
- Army Corps of Engineers–Seattle, WA
- Army Corps of Engineers–Walla Walla, WA
- Department of Energy–Richland, WA
- Department of Transportation – USCG – Seattle, WA
- Fairchild AFB–Spokane, WA
- Ft. Lewis–Tacoma, WA
- General Services Administration–Auburn, WA
- McChord AFB–Tacoma, WA
- Naval Supply Center–Bremerton, WA
- Naval Facilities Engineering Command - Silverdale, WA

Acquisition Team Facilitators Impart *Gems of Wisdom*

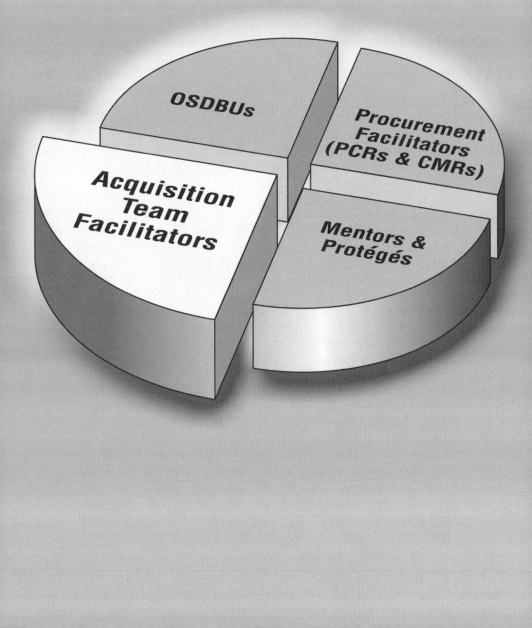

Acquisition Team Facilitators
Impart *Gems of Wisdom*

Mastering the information contained in the previous chapters will prepare 8(a)BD firms to have productive and positive interchanges with acquisition team members.

A good working knowledge of contract types, of basic principles and rules of accounting for government contracts, and of the requirements of cost proposal preparation is essential. You don't need to be an expert but you must understand the fundamentals. When in doubt don't guess, seek expert advice.

It's difficult to get a foot in the door but when people believe in you they will help you get through. 8(a)BD firm owners should strive to make a positive impression first with their Business Opportunity Specialist, then with the OSDBUs, PCRs and CMRs. Each one of these business development facilitators are in a position to help you get in the door to meet program and contracting officers—but they won't go the extra mile for you unless they perceive that you are a "winner." As the saying goes, "Everybody loves a winner."

To be a winner and to create a positive impression there are two things an 8(a)BD firm owner must do: First, they must be able to succinctly convey information about the firm's successful past performance. Secondly, they must demonstrate that they understand the rules and regulations of the federal government marketplace and have set up internal management systems to comply with them.

It's especially important for 8(a)BD firm in the Development Stage to demonstrate knowledge about government contracting to begin to build confidence among business development facilitators. In addition, when firms in this stage can confidently assert "this is what our firm does and although we haven't yet done it in the federal environment, here's where we did it, and here's precisely where our experience matches the following needs in the federal contracting environment..."it makes a positive impression. It's equally important for 8(a)BD firms in the Transition Stage to demonstrate knowledge of the dynamics of the federal marketplace and to demonstrate that they are constantly upgrading their systems to comply with government rules. By so doing, they position themselves to receive larger contracts.

There's a lot implied in the foregoing and a lot that has to happen in the background before an 8(a) firm can be in a position to provide reassurances not only about the firm's technical capabilities, but about the firm owner's knowledge of how the federal marketplace works. Studying government contracting rules is a must and ongoing exercise. Studying procurement forecasts is also a must, and maintaining constant contact with all key players in the business development network to let them know about what the firm has done and can do is highly advisable.

> Knowledge is one thing but putting knowledge into production is another. Nothing is a better demonstration of having done so than having one's accounting house in order. If there was one *"gem of wisdom"* that stood out above all others from among successful 8(a)BD graduates interviewed for the first *"Gems"* book, it was that they placed equal emphasis on establishing the internal infrastructure for the firm as they did on developing the technical offerings of the firm.

Adherence to government accounting principles gives 8(a)BD firms the key to the kingdom. It's the one thing, above all others, which gives the most comfort and reassurance that firm owners know what they are doing. Nobody wants to deal with a firm that could get in an embarrassing situation by not knowing the rules. Having the most technically qualified staff doesn't alone provide the comfort or reassurance that is required in a federal government contracting environment. What provides comfort is the belief that the firm's technical qualifications are matched by operational knowledge of federal government contracting and by having internal management systems in place that ensure compliance.

With this background the stage is set for a discussion about how to interact with members of the acquisition team.

For starters, it should be recognized that along with tremendous growth in the amount of contracting is an increase in the proportion of contracts being used to purchase more complex products and services, and in the proportion of contracts for services.

The government no longer contracts for just office supplies, facility support, and production of ships, planes and major weapon systems; today, the government uses contractors to provide complex consulting (such as technology support and financial system development), and highly complex research and development services. In some contracts, the government works in partnership with the contractor to develop cutting edge solutions to rapidly developing problems.

Although contracting has become more costly and more complex, the number of contracting officers available to work on contracts, according to the U.S. Merit Systems Protection Board's report on *Contracting Officer Representatives* in 2005, remained stagnant from 1997 to 2004.

What does this mean to the 8(a)BD firm? It means that 8(a)BD firms must recognize that contracting and program officers are under a lot of stress; therefore, the more the firm knows about the contracting process the better. In addition, better contracting outcomes results when contractors are knowledgeable about the rules. Secondly, as the practice of bundling contracts is taker a firmer hold, 8(a)BD firms must constantly search for partners in order to be included in larger contracts. Most importantly, 8(a)BD firms must perform well when they do get an opportunity.

Understanding How The Acquisition Team Works

First and foremost, it should be understood that contractors are part of the acquisition team, along with program and contract officers. They should make sure that they are not the weakest link in the chain.

Contracting—also called procurement or acquisition—is a significant and complex government activity involving employees at all levels and from a number of different occupations. It varies in complexity depending on a number of factors including the type of the contract and the agency procurement process, systems, and culture within which contracting is conducted.

Contract administration varies from contract to contract. It can range from the minimum acceptance of a delivery and payment to the contractor to extensive involvement by program, audit, and procurement officials throughout the contract term.

Factors influencing the degree of contract administration include the nature of the work, the type of contract, and the experience and commitment of the personnel involved. Contract administration starts with developing clear, concise performance based statements of work to the extent possible, and preparing a contract administration plan that cost effectively measures the contractor's performance and provides documentation to pay accordingly.

Members of the Acquisition Team

The "acquisition team" consists of all participants in the acquisition process including government employees ranging from senior agency leaders to administrative and support employees; it also includes contractors. The roles of three key groups on the acquisition team—Program Managers, Contract Officers (COs), Contract Officer Representatives (CORs) are discussed below.

Program managers generally know what is needed by their organization and why, and are responsible for certifying that there is a legitimate need for the products or services to be covered by the contract. In addition, program managers authorize the program funds to pay for the item. Program managers are the customers and their needs drive the procurement process.

Procurement professionals, primarily COs, serve as the Government's "agent" and are responsible for the business aspects of the contract and for ensuring adherence to procurement laws and the regulations contained in the FAR.13. In contracting, the "law of agency" refers to one party (the principal) who appoints another party (the agent) to enter into a business or contractual relationship with a third party (the contractor). The Government is the principal, the contracting officer is the agent, and the contractor is the third party.

COs usually work in the procurement office rather than the program office and provide the expertise on the business aspects of the contracting process. The FAR provides criteria for the selection of a CO based on the complexity and dollar value of the acquisitions (contracts) to be assigned and the candidate's experience, training, education, business acumen, judgment, character, and reputation. He or she is responsible for ensuring performance of all necessary contracting actions, compliance with the terms of the contract, and safeguarding the interests of the United States in its contractual relationships. Legally, it is the CO, as the Government's agent, who is responsible for ensuring the integrity of the contracting process.

COs may, but rarely do, possess sufficient expertise in the functional area of the contract to manage or oversee the contract's technical aspects. Therefore, it is common for the CO to delegate the technical oversight and/ or administrative management aspects of the contracting process to the COR. Delegation of technical responsibilities to the COR is also important in small agencies where one or two COs cannot possess all of the technical expertise required to develop and oversee all of the agency's contracts. In reality, a small agency may have a need to purchase nearly as many different products and services as a large agency.

The CORs usually work in the **program office**—the functional organization that needs a product or service provided by the contract. CORs provide the technical and program expertise necessary to develop and manage the contract. Procurement policy specifically includes CORs (or **Contract Officer's Technical Representatives—COTRs**) and other equivalent positions as part of the minimal definition of the acquisition workforce. CORs are usually selected by or with the advice of the program office. In addition, CORs only have authority to work on contracts to the degree they have been formally delegated such authority by the CO.

> While the FAR provides guidance and criteria for the selection of COs, *it provides no such guidance or criteria for the selection of CORs. Therefore, the process of COR selection (and assignment) varies greatly from agency to agency.* Agencies may select CORs based on their expertise in a technical or functional area, experience, training, knowledge of contracting rules or procedures, or the complexity or dollar value of the contract. However, agencies are not required to use these or any other criteria as the basis for selecting or assigning CORs.

The foregoing sheds light on why it's so difficult to identify a list of CORs or COTRs in an agency: There is no predetermined list. As stated above, their selection varies from agency to agency and is based on the nature of the work involved in the procurement. Given this, an important research task for 8(a)BD firms is to identify who the COTRs or CORs are that are assigned to handle the procurements in which they have an interest. The forecast documents provided through the OSDBUs should contain this information. If it doesn't it is appropriate for firms to request the assistance of the OSDBU to identify such persons.

The Contracting Process and the Role of CORs (or COTRs)

Contracting is usually carried out in three stages—**contract planning, contract formation**, and **contract management**. Figure 1, as described by U.S. Merit Systems Protection Board's 2005 study on contacting officer representatives, depicts this process.

The contract planning stage begins when a program manager or executive (the contract customer) decides that the Government needs a product and/or a service and ends with determining the terms and conditions of the solicitation (the notice to contractors to apply for a government contract). The contract formation stage begins with the formal solicitation for offers or bids and ends with a signed contract awarded to the contractor with the best proposal. The contract management stage begins with the initiation of work on the contract and ends with contract closeout or termination.

Figure 1: The Contracting Process

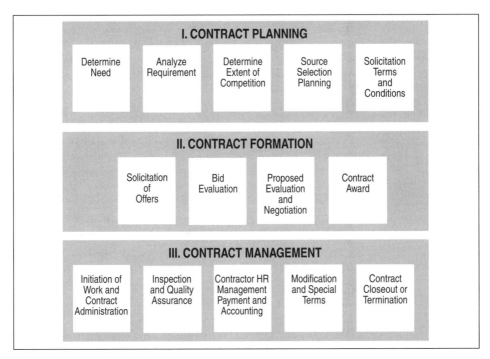

Attention is drawn to one very important thing that happens in Part II, which is the post-award orientation. It happens either by conference, letter or some other form of communication. Ideally, it should be the beginning of the process of good contract administration. This communication process can be a useful tool that helps government and contractor achieve a clear and mutual understanding of the contract requirements. It also helps the contractor understand the roles and responsibilities of the government officials who will administer the contract, and reduces future problems.

It's also helpful to have a "pre-meeting" with applicable program and contracting officials prior to the post award orientation conference so that there's a clear understanding of their specific responsibilities and restrictions in administering the contract. Items that should be discussed at the pre-meeting include such things as the authority of government personnel who will administer the contract, quality control and testing, the specific contract deliverable requirements, special contract provisions, the government's procedures for monitoring and measuring performance, contractor billing, voucher approval, and payment procedures.

Figure 2 provides delineates some of the common tasks that CORs perform in the contracting process organized according to the stages of contracting. This listing provides a good overview of the technical aspects of contracting and the important role that CORs play in successful contracting.

Figure 2: Contract Planning

CONTRACT PLANNING
• Advise on or determine a need for a product or service
• Analyze technical requirements of the product or service
• Conduct market research to establish technical requirements or identify potential contracts
• Provide technical information to assist in determining type of contract and level of competition
• Plan the technical aspects of the source selection process
• Establish the solicitation's technical terms and conditions
• Help prepare the statement of work (SOW) and other terms and conditions of the solicitation

CONTRACT FORMATION
• Serve on panels to evaluate bids and proposals
• Establish the contract's technical terms and conditions

CONTRACT MANAGEMENT

Administration
- Serve as agency's technical representative for contract administration
- Represent agency in technical meetings, record important facts
- Confer with program office and user groups on contract performance
- Maintain COR file
- Assist contractor in understanding technical requirements

Monitoring the technical work of the contractor, quality assurance and inspection of deliverables
- Determine and list the deliverables required from the contractor, with due dates
- Monitor the contractor's compliance with submitting deliverables
- Review and approve or reject technical deliverables
- Give technical direction to contractor
- Ensure all work is in accordance with the contract requirements
- Review and monitor progress reports and work plans
- Ensure the contractor is complying with its quality control systems
- Advise the CO of work that is accepted or rejected
- Ensure the contractor properly corrects all defects and omissions

Changes and modifications
- Advise the CO of the need to issue change orders, develop estimates for equitable adjustments, assist in evaluating contractor claims
- Perform a technical review of contractor proposed changes

Contractor human resources management and financial management issues
- Ensure contractor exhibits required materials for EEO, contract laws, and job safety
- Report violations of labor standards to the CO
- Monitor time worked and contractor record-keeping procedures
- Ensure contractor enforces all health and safety requirements
- Ensure contractor assigns employees with the necessary capabilities, qualifications, and experience
- Review and quickly process contractor invoices
- Determine if progress or advance payment requests should be processed

Contract closeout or termination
- Provide technical information for contract termination decisions
- Forward COR file to CCO when COR duties end

Much is implied in the foregoing. A detailed discussion of what it entails from the COR (COTR's) perspective is discussed below.

Contract Planning

COR involvement in contract planning is important to ensure that the contract accurately and completely delineates the government's technical needs and how the deliverables will be assessed to determine if they meet those needs.

In the contract planning stage, CORs work with program managers to determine whether there is a need for the Government to contract for a particular product or service. Then, CORs work with COs to conduct a more detailed analysis of the needs, including defining the technical requirements or performance standards the contract must meet. CORs also help establish the initial timeframes for the contract because they know when the deliverable must be provided and/or how long a deliverable could take to be produced. COR input regarding the contract timeframes is especially important if the deliverable is a subcomponent of a larger agency initiative with which the COR is thoroughly familiar.

In the first **Gems of Wisdom** (2007) book, successful 8(a)BD graduate Rodney Hunt indicated that one of the biggest contract losses he incurred while in the program was in a situation where the Government didn't know what it wanted but issued a fixed-price contract for the work, which he accepted. According to Hunt, it was a big mistake for him to accept such an ill-defined TOR on a firm fixed-fee basis because the client kept making him develop different scenarios.

CORs help the CO determine the appropriate type of contract to allow the Government to obtain what it needs at a reasonable cost and at an acceptable level of risk.

The type of contract chosen determines the appropriate level of competition and negotiation and the pricing structure of the contract.

Contract types can range from the simple purchase of commercial products (e.g., office supplies) to long-term research and development services (e.g., advanced technical system design and testing) to capital construction (e.g., building courthouses, prisons or roads). There are certain types of contracts, such as those for major research and development services that are particularly difficult to develop and manage. For these kinds of contracts, the Government may not know what the final product or service should look like or how it should perform because of rapidly changing needs or technology. Instead, the product or service is developed in partnership with the contractor, which makes the involvement of highly skilled Government employees even more important to ensuring positive outcomes.

Commercial, fixed-price contracts, by contrast, such as those used to purchase office supplies or facilities maintenance services, typically have price ranges associated with specific levels of quality and quantity that have been established over time to the point of becoming recognized standards. Commercial, fixed-price contracts do not typically require complex negotiation to obtain a fair price for the Government and several contractors are usually able to provide competitive prices. The risk to the Government is reduced because it is easier to show when a commercial item does or does not meet established standards. The involvement of CORs is useful in these types of contracts to ensure that the appropriate quality of the commercial product is obtained at an appropriate cost.

Contracts designed to purchase complex professional services, major integrated hardware systems, research and development services, or construction services are particularly complex. These types of contracts typically have variable, "cost-plus" pricing structures where the amount paid to the contractor is the cost of goods (raw materials or supplies) plus the cost of the level of effort the contractor spends to accomplish the work.

> But in Hunt's case, he made a mistake by accepting a fixed-fee contract instead of a "cost-plus" contract to design a major IT system.

> Performance-based contracts: In this type of contract, the Government specifies the performance standards that the contract deliverables have to meet—such as what the deliverable must do and how well they have to do it—and sets a fixed price for the contract. The process or approach used to achieve the performance standards is the responsibility of the contractor. If the costs are more than anticipated, the contractor absorbs the additional cost. In this way, the financial risk shifts away from the Government and to the contractor. However, even in performance based contracts, determining the required performance standards of the deliverables (developing performance metrics) requires the technical expertise provided by CORs.

Often the level of effort is not known at the beginning of the contract. In addition, in complex, cutting-edge research and development contracts, the Government may not always know what the optimal deliverable of the contract should look like. In such cases, the overall costs cannot be well estimated, and the risk of contract failure is borne by the government in those instances when more money must be paid to compensate contractors required to put in more effort than was initially estimated. Given the level of uncertainty in estimating final costs and the risks to the Government, the role of the COR is essential in these types of contracts. Under these circumstances, the COR plans the technical aspects of the contract, anticipates the risk and potential challenges the contractor and the Government may face and how those risks may be managed over time, and helps establish appropriate intervals and milestones for the contract.

During planning, CORs also work with the CO to develop the source selection process including the technical criteria for evaluating contractor's proposals. CORs may use their expertise and **familiarity with those contractors** to conduct market research to gather information about technical criteria, or to obtain a list of potential sources (contractors). The CO uses this information to promote competition and ensure the agency gets a sufficient number of high quality proposals from which to select a final contractor.

Finally, CORs work with the CO to prepare the terms and conditions of the solicitation—or the formal request for contractors to submit proposals to accomplish specified work for the Government. The Government's technical requirements are laid out in a statement of work (SOW). The SOW, along with the requirements for timeliness and anticipated cost and other information necessary for the contractors to understand the Government's requirements, make up the solicitation's terms and conditions. CORs provide the technical expertise necessary to convey the requirements in understandable and precise terms in the solicitation.

> Because CORs often turn to the contractors they know, it's important for 8(a)BD firms to be known to them.

> Pricing arrangements--are important because they partly determine how difficult the contract is to oversee. In addition, the pricing arrangement determines the relative risk placed on the Government or on the contractor should the contract fail. Fixed-price contracts are typically used to purchase commercial off-the-shelf products and services. In such contracts, the contractor bears most of the risk, and the oversight work is usually more straightforward. Fixed- price products and services usually have well-established, industry-wide, easily measured standards that require little or no judgment on the part of the COR in terms of meeting requirements. Other, more complex types of pricing arrangements—such as "cost plus effort," or "time and materials" pricing, are not based on straightforward fixed-prices. There are many options for pricing arrangements from fixed-price to cost reimbursable, to indefinite delivery/indefinite quantity (IDIQ), to performance based, to any combination of arrangements.

Contract Formation

The contract formation phase begins with the formal solicitation for proposals and ends with awarding the contract. The solicitation is published in a "request for proposal" or "request for bid" to inform potential contractors (those who wish to provide the product or service to the Government) of the Government's needs for goods and/or services. The solicitation is the basis on which contractors "propose" to the Government how and what they will provide, when they will provide it, and at what cost. If significant aspects of the requirements were overlooked or not sufficiently specified in the contract planning phase, then the contract formation phase will probably not result in a contract that can accomplish the work intended.

The technical assessment of the contract proposal is the primary activity of CORs during this phase. Once proposals or bids are received, they are evaluated against a pre-established set of criteria to determine which contractor offers the best value for the Government. CORs are helpful in interpreting or assessing the proposals to determine which ones provide complete information from which to judge the capability of the contractor. CORs should also be involved in assessing contractor proposals to ensure that the technical criteria for bid evaluation established during contract planning are accurately and completely applied and that any technical issues are resolved so that each contractor can compete fully and fairly for the Government's business. CORs may also serve on panels established to provide formal review and rating of proposals.

Often, CORs are involved with the CO in negotiations between the Government and the contractor(s) to ensure that the final agreement will meet the Government's technical requirements and be satisfactory to all parties. CORs may be involved in other contract activities during contract formation including investigating contractor past performance and providing input for estimating contract costs. The contract formation stage results in a signed contract between the Government and a specified contractor or contractors. This contract should clearly and completely lay out the Government's requirements, the roles of both the contractor and the Government, and the means to effectively assess that the requirements (*quality, timeliness, completeness,* and *cost*) are met.

Contract Management

The next stage of the contract is the contract management phase. This phase begins with the initiation of work by the contractor and ends with the closeout or termination of the contract. The goal of this phase is to ensure the contractor meets the Government's technical requirements for quality and completeness, at the cost, and within the timeframes established by the contract. Assuming a well-developed contract, the success of the contract depends on the contractor's performance in delivering services and products and the Government's performance in monitoring the contract and assessing that these technical requirements are met.

CORs generally perform this technical oversight function because they are usually the only people with the expertise and position within the agency to assess the contractor's performance. Typical activities in the contract management phase include initiation of work and administration of the contract, monitoring the technical work of the contractor (including quality assurance and inspection of deliverables), contractor HR management and payment and accounting of contract funds, modification of the contract, satisfying any special terms of the contract, and closeout or termination of the contract.

> **Definition of success:** If the contract succeeds, it means that the contractor has produced the products and services required, and that the representative—the COR—accurately and effectively judged that the products and services satisfy the requirements in terms of quality, timelines, completeness, and cost. It also means that in the end, the Government has gotten what it needs, and the contractor is paid a fair price for those deliverables. In other words, the contractor did what was expected and the Government's representatives did their job in overseeing and certifying the contractor's work.

Contract management is the most critical phase from the program office's perspective because it is during this phase that **the contract will either succeed or fail to satisfy the Government's requirements**.

It's important to note that contract management is often extremely challenging and problems in managing contracts can result in the failure of the contract. CORs are intimately involved in all parts of contract management, but their key responsibility is to ensure that all the technical issues of the contract are managed effectively.

> The hope is that any contract difficulties would be minor and easily resolved. However, when the contract deliverables significantly fail to meet the technical requirements, are not timely, are not complete, or are more costly than originally agreed upon, then the Government or the contractor must take action to correct the situation.

CORs must work hand-in-hand with the CO to resolve any problems that arise. Technical issues in contract management such as monitoring contractor performance, judging the quality of deliverables, and knowing when contracts should be modified are complex issues. Inspection standards for some products and deliverables are well-established, but standards for more complex deliverables may have to be created for each contract. More complex and costly contracts, or contracts that require more judgment on the part of the COR, make the COR's job more difficult.

Regardless of the cause of the problem, or who takes the action, the problem is likely to increase costs to the Government and to reduce the chances for a successful outcome.

The final activities in contract management involve closing out or terminating the contract—each of which requires different but important work for the CORs. If the contractor was successful in meeting the Government's requirements, the contract is closed out.

Close-out activities include certifying completion of all deliverables, reviewing and storing records used during the contract, and completing the final payments to the contractor. A contract can also be terminated before its completion. If there were significant problems during the execution of the contract resulting in the contractor's failure to perform, the contract can be terminated for cause. Alternately, if the Government's requirements have changed significantly, the contract can be terminated based on those changing needs. Termination of contracts may require more work for the COR, such as providing evidence of technical insufficiency and furnishing other administrative documentation that will withstand contract review, as well as audit and appeals procedures. The purpose is to end the contract and minimize the cost to the Government, as failed contracts often require additional effort and money to hire a new contractor to complete or redo the work.

Advice of Acquisition Team Members

The bottom line is: All members of the acquisition team want the contract to succeed. Therefore, all members must do their part to ensure its success.

Failure is not an option for the 8(a)BD firm is today's fiercely competitive environment.

There are four desired outcomes CORs are looking for in order to conclude that contract performance has been successful. They are:

- Quality
- Timeliness
- Completeness
- Cost

Quite simply, did the 8(a)BD firm deliver the expected quality of product? Did the firm provide the goods or services on time? Did the firm do a thorough and complete job? And, did the firm perform the project within the budgeted costs? When firms fail on any one of these measures, that's not a good thing.

Anecdotal discussions with a sample of COs, CORs (or COTRs), and program officers in different agencies indicate that, in many cases, contracts tend to fail to achieve at least one of the four desired outcomes in terms of quality, timeliness, completeness, and cost. For each of these four categories, individually, some estimate that approximately 75 percent of contract deliverables tend to meet the goal.

The objective of an 8(a)BD contractor should be to meet all of the desired contract outcomes.

According to acquisition team members in different agencies, one of the areas that tends to trip up 8(a)BD firms is having poorly established indirect cost rates. When firms don't have a firm handle on their cost structures they tend to underbid jobs and then run into trouble before the job is completed. Therefore, an important *gem of wisdom* to pass on to 8(a)BD firms is to pay attention to their indirect costing.

What are indirect costs? Indirect costs are costs which cannot be directly identified with a single contract or grant. The indirect costs are applied equitably across all of the business activities of the organization, according to the benefits each gains from them. Some examples of indirect costs are office space rental, utilities, and clerical and managerial staff salaries. To the extent that indirect costs are reasonable, allowable and allocable they are a legitimate cost of doing business payable under a U.S. Government contract or grant.

How are rates are established? Responsibility for negotiating indirect cost rates with organizations doing business with the U.S. Government is specifically assigned. Each organization negotiates its indirect cost rates with one government agency that has been assigned cognizance. Usually the cognizant government agency is that agency which has the largest dollar volume of contracts with the firm or organization. The resulting Negotiated Indirect Cost Rate Agreement (NICRA) is binding on the entire government.

The NICRA contains both final rates for past periods and provisional (billing rates) for current and future periods. A procurement office **may not negotiate a different rate or base of application** for an individual cost reimbursement contract or program. The provisional (billing) rate is established for use in reimbursing indirect costs under cost-reimbursement contracts and grants until a final rate can be established. The billing rate may be revised by the cognizant agency to prevent substantial overpayment or underpayment in the event of a significant change in the firm's business volume, but should not be revised during individual contract or grant negotiations. A final indirect cost rate is established after the close of the contractor's fiscal year and once established is not subject to change. For more information see:
http://www.arnet.gov/far/current/html/Subpart%2042_7.html

An example of comparative costs between different organizations is shown below.

Comparative Costs Between Organizations		
Cost Elements	**Company ABC**	**Company XYZ**
Direct Labor	$100,000	$100,000
Fringe Benefits	$ 25,000	$ 25,000
Subtotal	$125,000	$125,000
Travel/Per Diem	$ 80,000	$ 80,000
Other Direct Cost	$200,000	$200,000
Equipment	$ 40,000	$ 40,000
Subcontracts	$ 50,000	$ 50,000
Total Direct		
Program Cost	$495,000	$495,000
Indirect Cost		
at 75%	$ 75,000	
at 25%		$123,750
Total Cost	**$570,000**	**$618,750**

Company ABC's rate applies to direct labor
Company XYZ's rate applies to total direct costsw

As can be seen in this comparison, the lowest rate does not necessarily result in the lowest indirect costs applicable to an award.

Good Common Sense Advice

There is a time and place for everything, but simplicity and solid execution always makes sense.

At the end of the day, there's no substitute for good old plain common sense. A lot of the problems that COs, CORs, and program officers have encountered when working with 8(a)BD firms could have been avoided through applying plain old common sense. Accordingly, firms should bear the following common sense guidelines in mind.

- **Good Government Contractors Facilitate Good Communication**: Determine early on the best method of communication, whether it's regular phone calls, faxes, email, on-site visits or a combination of these.

- **Good Government Contractors Understand Agency Requirements:** Make sure you stay on top of agency requirements, changes in the rules, etc. Maintaining open lines of communication between government contractors and contracting officials will certainly help. However, you should also monitor the FAR website for news about changes to government contracting laws and regulations. Don't be caught off-guard.

■ **Good Government Contractors Are Flexible:** Consider partnering with other government contractors on contracts. Some government jobs may require skills or products that your business won't be able to provide, and that's acceptable as long as you find a partner to fill in the gaps. Just be sure to draw up a contract with the subcontractor that specifies payment and responsibilities so there are no misunderstandings.

■ **Good Government Contractors Document Everything:** Document each step of the process and keep thorough written records throughout the project, and for years thereafter. File everything from timesheets to memos for future reference and to avoid disputes. From beginning to end, government contractors should seize every opportunity to make a good impression. Make sure the government has a go-to person for every phase of the project. Your commitment and enthusiasm should be as strong on the last day of the contract as it was on the first.

■ **Good Government Contractors Always Meet Deadlines:** Make your deadlines, and deliver the goods or services as promised. Let officials know of your prior experience as government contractors. Prospective purchasers might ask for references, too, so be prepared to provide them with a list of contacts. Word of mouth can be one of your best marketing tools.

■ **Good Government Contractors Know Their Costs and How to Manage Them**: Your ability to meet your indirect cost rates is extremely important. The easiest way to track rate performance is to track and manage your labor utilization rate (the percentage determined by dividing billable labor by total labor) each pay period and year-to-date. This is because direct labor is the primary driver of your indirect cost rates. A good labor utilization rate might be 85%. You should know yours intimately.

■ **Good Government Contractors Base Their Prices on Their Costs:** Once you establish a certain pricing structure for your company, it will be very difficult to negotiate a higher one. Remember that later, when you try to negotiate your true (higher) costs, the negotiator you are dealing with will have to explain why, under his or her watch, the cost of your services grew by XX%. Accordingly, if you must lower your costs to win a contract, the best place to achieve the savings is in lower direct costs. This is especially true if you know that your competition's indirect cost load (which is to say their pricing) is similar to yours.

- **Good Government Contractors Know That Profits Come From Well-Negotiated Fees**: Experienced contractors recognize that the real rewards in government contracting come not from contract fees, but from above the line profits: those that can be safely taken as allowable costs through various fringe benefit plans. If there ever was a good reason to control other Overhead and G&A costs, being able to contribute more to these plans is one. If you are just starting out, include as many of these benefits in your indirect cost budget as you reasonably can. You'll never regret it!

- **Good Government Contractors Know How to Plan in Advance in Moving to a New Accounting System**: When you decide to move to a new accounting system and purchase new software, it's critical that you get "up-and-running" as soon as possible. While this may seem obvious, in moving to new software numerous obstacles to implementation may emerge. The best approach is to get the new software up and running then to "fine tune" it later. If you have selected the correct software, it should enhance the capabilities of your firm.

- **Good Government Contractors Have Well Qualified Accountants and Contract Negotiators:** If something doesn't "sound" right about the contractual terms, it probably isn't. To avoid problems down the road, have your team of experts review the matter before committing the firm.

Chapter Four imparts *gems of wisdom* of Mentors and Protégés.

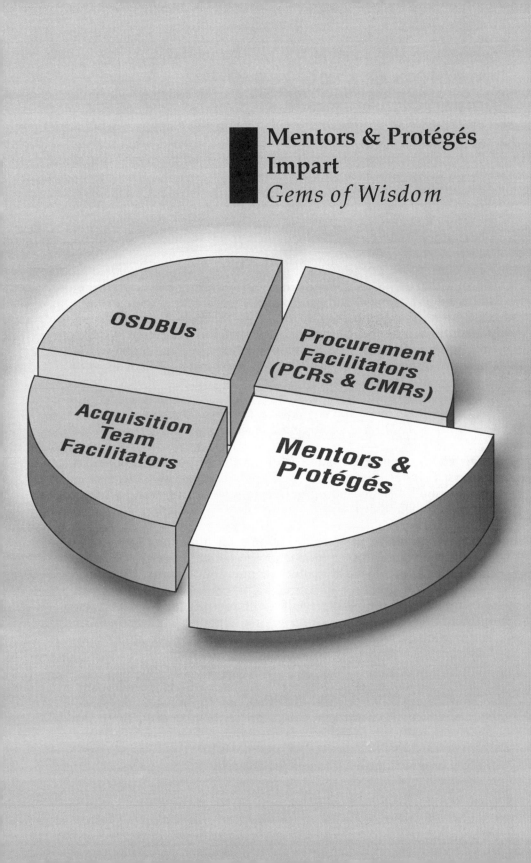

Mentors & Protégés Impart
Gems of Wisdom

OSDBUs

Procurement Facilitators (PCRs & CMRs)

Acquisition Team Facilitators

Mentors & Protégés

Mentors & Protégés
Impart *Gems of Wisdom*

The 8(a) Mentor-Protégé program is the jewel in the crown among all business development resources.

When 8(a)BD firms take full advantage of all of the business development resources that are made available to them chances are that they will be ready to embark upon a mutually beneficial Mentor-Protégé relationship.

Throughout this book the importance of acquiring and acting upon knowledge has been underscored. Evidence that firms have put the knowledge they have gained into production is demonstrated when they know the rules, develop internal management systems to comply with them, and develop a positive reputation based on the quality of their performance. Business development experts have noted:

> *"Corporate reputation impacts business results and as such should be treated with as much vigor as other business risk."*

Faye Fields, one of the successful 8(a)BD graduates profiled in the first *Gems of Wisdom* book perhaps put it best when she said, in a nutshell: "Firms should gain a reputation for doing what is required to help them win."

The list of potential 8(a) protégés from which mentors can choose is long. Why and how mentors choose one 8(a) firm over another as a protégé has a lot to do with the reputation the firm has gained. The same rules that apply to managing corporate reputations in a commercial environment apply to emerging 8(a) firms that are primarily working in the federal government marketplace. In other words, *how* 8(a)BD firms do what they do, and the reputation they leave behind after having done it, matters.

The 8(a) Mentor-Protégé program, as one business development vehicle, is arguably the resource that has the most potential to help advance 8(a) firms and help prepare them to compete in the American economy in the long term. Protégés have to be ready for the relationship, however. We are reminded that the purpose of the 8(a)BD program, among other objectives, is to:

- Promote the business development of small business concerns owned and controlled by socially and economically disadvantaged individuals so that such concerns can compete on an equal basis in the American economy;

- Promote the competitive viability of such concerns in the marketplace by providing such available contract, financial, technical, and management assistance as may be necessary.

In any situation where a firm is being given a "hand up," one hand reaches down to pull up the firm, while the hand of the other firm reaches up. The measure of the extent to which a firm is reaching upward is the firm's reputation. Therefore, before discussing the details of the Mentor-Protégé, it's useful to discuss the importance of a firm's reputation.

What Influences Corporate Reputation?

In 2003, Hill & Knowlton and Korn/Ferry issued its *International Corporate Reputation Watch* (CRW) report. One of its main findings was that most CEOs in top corporations believed that a company's corporate reputation was considerably more important to the company today than in the past. Specifically, the report found:

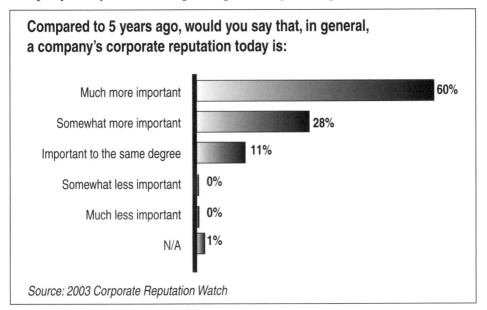

Compared to 5 years ago, would you say that, in general, a company's corporate reputation today is:

Much more important — 60%
Somewhat more important — 28%
Important to the same degree — 11%
Somewhat less important — 0%
Much less important — 0%
N/A — 1%

Source: 2003 Corporate Reputation Watch

In answering the question of what's at stake if a firm's reputation fails, the study found:

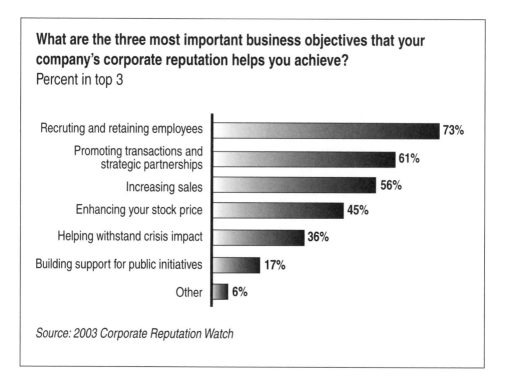

What are the three most important business objectives that your company's corporate reputation helps you achieve?
Percent in top 3

Objective	Percent
Recruiting and retaining employees	73%
Promoting transactions and strategic partnerships	61%
Increasing sales	56%
Enhancing your stock price	45%
Helping withstand crisis impact	36%
Building support for public initiatives	17%
Other	6%

Source: 2003 Corporate Reputation Watch

Attention is drawn to the impact of reputation on promoting strategic partnerships. Relating this to the 8(a) Mentor-Protégé realm, it could equally be argued that a bad reputation reduces the probability that an 8(a) firm will be selected by a mentor, and the converse is also true. Importantly, the report also concluded that:

A company's reputation is the *external* manifestation of its people, internal practices, culture, management talent, and overall competitiveness. These are the critical factors that determine the leaders and laggards in the world of business.

The mechanisms through which quality employees yield good customers, increased sales, etc. are well known. In other words, more effective employees can mean better products and services, more efficient operations, more positive "moments of truth" in customer interactions, and so on. Further, it's not just a person-to-person, employee-to-customer event that induces positive business results—for example, positive media coverage can intermediate as well by spreading the word about the firm.

The "internal" aspect of reputation management is equally important but often overlooked. Individual pride in the organization depends on what management does and on the structure of the organization, and the clarity of its goals and values.

A model put forth in the CRW (2003) report illustrates the linkages among employees, organizational practices, customers, reputation, and business success. The model provides a partial picture of what is believed by business leaders to produce corporate reputation and what they believe it can accomplish.

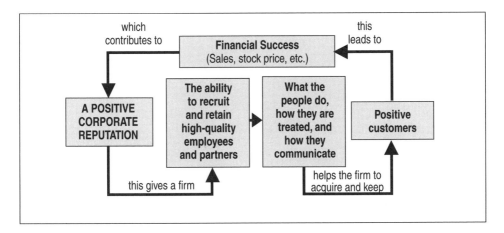

Finally, the CRW report underscores that firms have multiple stakeholder audiences that are central to their reputation. Among them, besides customers and employees, are *strategic alliance partners*, shareholders, regulators, competitors, media, and others that may be specific to a company or its industry. The relative centrality of each of these to the reputation of a given firm in a given industry will vary, and should be understood early in any assessment of corporate reputation. A stakeholder "reputation" matrix was put forward in the report, which is shown below.

Reputation clearly matters, and it especially matters in terms of influencing a potential mentor's decision about which 8(a) firm to select as a protégé. Firms seeking to be mentored should ask themselves if their reputation is good enough to attract a mentor. If the answer is yes, there's a lot to learn about how to make the relationship work.

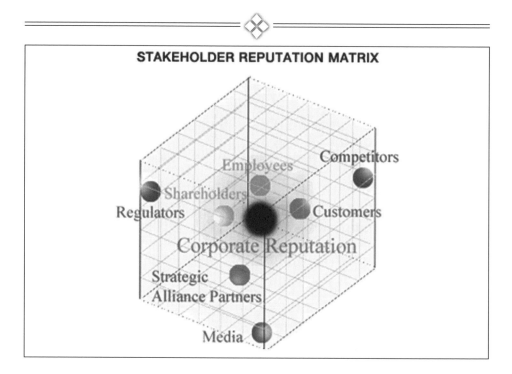

STAKEHOLDER REPUTATION MATRIX

Mentoring and Protégé-*ing*

The starting place in any discussion about federal programs is always about the rules. Accordingly, the rules of that govern SBA's 8(a) Mentor-Protégé program are shown in Box 5.

Box 5:
Sec. 124.520 Mentor/Protégé Program

(a) General. The mentor/protégé program is designed to encourage approved mentors to provide various forms of assistance to eligible Participants. This assistance may include technical and/or management assistance; financial assistance in the form of equity investments and/or loans; subcontracts; and/ or assistance in performing prime contracts with the Government in the form of joint venture arrangements. The purpose of the mentor/protégé relationship is to enhance the capabilities of the protégé and to improve its ability to successfully compete for contracts.

(b) Mentors. Any concern that demonstrates a commitment and the ability to assist developing 8(a) Participants may act as a mentor and receive benefits as set forth in this section. This includes businesses that have graduated from the 8(a) BD program, firms that are in the transitional stage of program participation, other small businesses, and large businesses.

(1) **In order to qualify as a mentor**, a concern must demonstrate that it:
    (i) possesses favorable financial health, including profitability for at least the last two years;

(ii) Possesses good character;

(iii) Does not appear on the federal list of debarred or suspended contractors; and

(iv) Can impart value to a protégé firm due to lessons learned and practical experience gained because of the 8(a) BD program, or through its general knowledge of government contracting.

(2) Generally, a mentor will have no more than one protégé at a time. However, the AA/8(a)BD may authorize a concern to mentor more than one protégé at a time where the concern can demonstrate that the additional mentor/protégé relationship will not adversely affect the development of either protégé firm (e.g., the second firm cannot be a competitor of the first firm).

(3) In order to demonstrate its favorable financial health, a firm seeking to be a mentor must submit its federal tax returns for the last two years to SBA for review.

(4) Once approved, a mentor must annually certify that it continues to possess good character and a favorable financial position.

(c) **Protégés**. (1) In order to initially qualify as a protégé firm, a Participant must:

(i)   Be in the developmental stage of program participation;

(ii)   Have never received an 8(a) contract; or

(iii) Have a size that is less than half the size standard corresponding to its primary SIC code.

(2) Only firms that are in good standing in the 8(a) BD program (e.g., firms that do not have termination or suspension proceedings against them, and are up to date with all reporting requirements) may qualify as a protégé.

(3) A protégé firm may have only one mentor at a time.

(d) **Benefits**. (1) A mentor and protégé may joint venture as a small business for any government procurement, including procurements less than half the size standard corresponding to the assigned SIC code and 8(a) sole source contracts, provided both the mentor and the protégé qualify as small for the procurement and, for purposes of 8(a) sole source requirements, the protégé has not reached the dollar limit set forth in Sec. 124.519.

(2) Notwithstanding the requirements set forth in Sec. 124.105(g) and (h), **in order to raise capital for the protégé firm, the mentor may own an equity interest of up to 40% in the protégé firm**.

(3) Notwithstanding the mentor/protégé relationship, a protégé firm may qualify for other assistance as a small business, including SBA financial assistance.

(4) **No determination of affiliation or control may be found between a protégé firm and its mentor based on the mentor/protégé agreement or any assistance provided pursuant to the agreement**.

(e) **Written agreement**. (1) The mentor and protégé firms must enter a written agreement setting forth an assessment of the protégé's needs and describing the assistance the mentor commits to provide to address those needs (e.g., management and/or technical assistance, loans and/or equity investments, cooperation on joint venture projects, or subcontracts under prime contracts being performed by the mentor). The agreement must also provide that the mentor will provide such assistance to the protégé firm for at least one year.

(2) The written agreement must be approved by the AA/8(a)BD. The agreement will not be approved if SBA determines that the assistance to be provided is not sufficient to promote any real developmental gains to the protégé, or if SBA determines that the agreement is merely a vehicle to enable a non-8(a) participant to receive 8(a) contracts.

(3) The agreement must provide that either the protégé or the mentor may terminate the agreement with 30 days advance notice to the other party to the mentor/protégé relationship and to SBA.

(4) SBA will review the mentor/protégé relationship annually to determine whether to approve its continuation for another year.

(5) SBA must approve all changes to a mentor/protégé agreement in advance.

(f) Evaluating the mentor/protégé relationship. (1) In its annual business plan update required by Sec. 124.403(a,) the protégé must report to SBA for the protégé's preceding program year:

(i)   All technical and/or management assistance provided by the mentor to the protégé;

(ii)   All loans to and/or equity investments made by the mentor in the protégé;

(iii) All subcontracts awarded to the protégé by the mentor, and the value of each subcontract;

(iv) All federal contracts awarded to the mentor/protégé relationship as a joint venture (designating each as an 8(a), small business set aside, or unrestricted procurement), the value of each contract, and the percentage of the contract performed and the percentage of revenue accruing to each party to the joint venture; and

(v) A narrative describing the success such assistance has had in addressing the developmental needs of the protégé and addressing any problems encountered.

(2) The protégé must annually certify to SBA whether there has been any change in the terms of the agreement.

(3) SBA will review the protégé's report on the mentor/protégé relationship as part of its annual review of the firm's business plan pursuant to Sec. 124.403. SBA may decide not to approve continuation of the agreement if it finds that the mentor has not provided the assistance set forth in the mentor/protégé agreement or that the assistance has not resulted in any material benefits or developmental gains to the protégé.

There's more here than may be obvious. In fact, enormous business development benefits are afforded through this program, which is why a number of federal government agencies have established their own programs. Although a number of such programs exist in different federal government agencies, arguably none are as advantageous to the protégé as the program created by the U.S. Small Business Administration (SBA).

As Verl Zanders observed, "The SBA Mentor-Protégé program is one of a kind; it allows Mentors to invest in the Protégé's firm without conflicting with the FAR affiliate rule."

To appreciate this *gem of wisdom*, it's important to understand the FAR affiliate rule. Accordingly, FAR 19.101 states:

"**Affiliates**." Business concerns are affiliates of each other if, directly or indirectly, either one controls or has the power to control the other, or another concern controls or has the power to control both. In determining whether affiliation exists, consideration is given to all appropriate factors including common ownership, common management, and contractual relationships; provided, that restraints imposed by a franchise agreement are not considered in determining whether the franchisor controls or has the power to control the franchisee, if the franchisee has the right to profit from its effort, commensurate with ownership, and bears the risk of loss or failure. Any business entity may be found to be an affiliate, whether or not it is organized for profit or located in the United States or its outlying areas. (1) *Nature of control.* Every business concern is considered as having one or more parties who directly or indirectly control or have the power to control it. Control may be affirmative or negative and it is immaterial whether it is exercised so long as the power to control exists.

SBA's Mentor-Protégé program provides an exception to the affiliate rule and permits mentors to "own an equity interest up to 40% in its Protégé firm." SBA summarizes the benefits of participating in its program as follows:

The Benefits of Participating in SBA's Mentor-Protégé Program: The Mentor and Protégé may joint venture as a small business for any government contract.

■ Expertise, resources and capabilities of the Mentor are made available to the 8(a) Participant Protégé;

■ To aid the Protégé to raise capital, (*e.g., Mentors may own an equity interest up to 40% in the Protégé firm*);

■ **No determination of affiliation or control may be found between a protégé firm and its mentor based on the mentor/protégé agreement** or any assistance provided pursuant to the agreement;

■ The Protégé, due to the additional capabilities gained from the Mentor, may better qualify for other assistance as a small business, including SBA financial assistance.

Accordingly, one of the most important *gems of wisdom* that can be imparted to 8(a)BD firms is to enter into a Mentor-Protégé program, if feasible, and if ready.

Information about SBA's Mentor-Protégé program, which can be found can be found on SBA's website, is summarized in Box 6. The information in the fact sheet is a simplification of the FAR rules, stated above, on the subject.

Box 6:
The Mentor-Protégé Fact Sheet

The SBA Mentor-Protégé Program is designed to encourage approved Mentors to provide various forms of assistance to eligible 8(a) Participants as Protégés. The purpose of the Mentor-Protégé relationship is to enhance the capabilities of the protégé and to improve its ability to successfully compete for Federal contracts. The various assistance that a Mentor may provide to a Protégé include:

- Technical and/or management assistance;

- Financial assistance in the form of equity investment, and/or loans;

- Offerings of subcontracts;

- Assistance in the performance of prime contracts with the Federal government in the form of Joint Venture arrangements.

The Small Business Administration (SBA) will administer the Mentor-Protégé Program. The SBA will determine the eligibility of participants in the Program, whether it be as Mentor, or as Protégé; will approve the Mentor-Protégé Agreement; will annually review existing Mentor-Protégé relationships: and, will serve as mediator of disputes between Mentor and Protégé.

Eligibility & Qualifications: Eligibility for participation in the Mentor-Protégé Program is subject to the approval of the SBA.

Mentors: To be eligible as a Mentor, a concern must demonstrate a commitment, and the ability to assist developing 8(a) Participants. The concern may have graduated from the 8(a) Program, or be in the Transitional Stage of the program. Other small businesses or large businesses with the same commitment and ability may also qualify to serve as Mentors. To qualify as a Mentor, a concern must demonstrate that it:

- Possesses a favorable financial health, including profitability for at least the last two years;

- Possesses a good character;

- Does not appear on the Federal list of Debarred or Suspended Contractors; and

- Can impart value to a Protégé firm due to lessons learned, and practical experience gained through the 8(a) Program, or from its general knowledge of government contracting.

Protégés: To initially qualify as a Protégé participant, a firm must:

- Be in the Developmental Stage of the 8(a) Program; or

- Have NOT yet received an 8(a) contract; or

- Have a size that is less than half the Size Standard corresponding to its primary SIC code.

The firm must also be in good standing in the 8(a) Program, i.e. the firm must not have termination or suspension proceedings against it, and is up-to-date with all reporting requirements.

A *Washington Technology* article in September 2007 by Michael Hardy emphasized the positive developmental benefits to 8(a)BD firms of participating in Mentor-Protégé arrangements, while advising firms to be smart about how they structure the relationship. A summary of the article is presented in Box 7.

Box 7:
2007 Small Business Report | Learning tree
Mentor/Protégé programs can help fledgling firms, but small companies need to be smart about using them

Many 8(a) companies eagerly enter mentor/protégé programs with larger firms hoping that they will earn revenues, learn business development skills, expand their market reach and lay a foundation for future growth.

Those programs are popular and often helpful, but smart businesses know how to avoid some common mistakes. As new players emerge and work their way toward becoming an established company's protégé, they should consider their motivations and expectations carefully, say some who have been there.

Many mentor/protégé programs exist in the government and are sponsored by various agencies. Although the details differ from one program to another, they are a way for disadvantaged small businesses, certified as such under Section 8(a) of the Small Business Act, to benefit from a close partnership with experienced companies.

But the programs are not meant primarily as a way to funnel contract revenues into the protégé companies, and companies who join them thinking they are mostly about earning subcontracts will struggle.

Tips for Mentor/Protégé Success

- The mentor/protégé relationship is about learning, not getting subcontracts. If you end up with some business in the bargain, count it as a bonus.

- Choose one goal to accomplish, such as setting up accounting processes that will pass federal muster or earning a CMMI rating.

- Be prepared to invest time and money. Count it as a short-term expense in exchange for a long-term gain.

- Take your mentor's guidance seriously. As the mentor has been successful in federal contracting and knows the business.

- Companies you've worked with in the past often make good mentors because there is already an established relationship to build on.

The aforementioned is deceptively simple. There's more here than meets the eye. For instance, there's a lot involved in earning a CMMI rating, and mentors can help protégés earn such ratings.

In 2004, Michael Hardy wrote an article explaining how important CMMI ratings are becoming in the government marketplace. He wrote:

Companies are in a never-ending quest to stand apart from the competition. As a means to that end, scores of certifications, ratings and credentials have sprung up that seek to provide companies and individuals with a stamp of approval of their ability and training. Systems integrators are eagerly pursuing a relatively new rating system.

The Capability Maturity Model Integration (CMMI) is replacing the older, well-established Capability Maturity Model ratings for software developers and systems engineers. Developed by the Software Engineering Institute at Carnegie Mellon University, CMMI covers a broader set of measures than CMM, including project management skills that are crucial to integrators. Similar to CMM, for which the institute no longer offers training, CMMI ratings range from Level 1 to Level 5 — Level 5 being the highest. They measure the degree of planning, documentation and discipline that a company exhibits.

Companies can receive ratings that apply to the whole firm, individual divisions or specific engagements. "It's really become the admission ticket to that [government] market," said Jay Douglass, director of business development at the institute. "If you're a federal government systems integrator, and you are not a minimum of Level 3, you're not given a lot of opportunity to bid." In turn, systems integrators increasingly use the ratings to evaluate potential suppliers and partners, he said. "It's a cascade from the government as a customer all the way down the supply chain..."

The foregoing underscores the importance of being competitive in today's terms, which is why having a mentor is perhaps more important than ever.

Strategic Considerations for Mentors and Protégés

Many strategic considerations are simply good common sense. Some advice, which is provided by the U.S. Small Business Administration (SBA), and which is shown on its website, falls into that category. According to SBA's advice:

Mentors:

- Provide guidance based on past business experiences;
- Create a positive counseling relationship and climate of open communication;
- Help protégés identify problems and solutions;
- Lead protégés through problem solving processes;
- Offer constructive criticism in a supportive way;
- Share stories, including mistakes;
- Assign "homework" if applicable;
- Refer protégés to other business associates;

- Solicit feedback from protégés;

- Come prepared to each meeting to discuss issues.

Protégés

- Shape the overall agenda for the relationship;

- Establish realistic and attainable expectations;

- Are open in communicating with the mentor;

- Establish priority issues for action or support;

- Don't expect the mentor to be an expert in all facets of business;

- Solicit feedback from your mentor;

- Come prepared to each meeting to discuss issues.

Mentors & Protégés

- Identify roles the mentor can play to help the protégé achieve goals;

- Develop an action plan to achieve agreed upon goals;

- Determine level of structure in the relationship;

- Communicate on a regular basis;

- Set milestones to monitor success of reaching goals;

- Set the agenda for each meeting;

- Schedule formal meetings and cancel only when absolutely necessary;

- Establish guidelines for telephone calls and other correspondence.

Finding a Mentor That's Right for You

- Look for a firm whose strategies and *modis operandi* you seek to model your firm on;

- Make sure the mentor you choose desires to be a mentor. A mentoring relationship requires consent by both parties;

- Look for what you can offer the mentor - make the relationship mutually beneficial.

Do(s) and Don't(s) for Mentors

Do(s)
- Be clear about your motives for helping your protégé. If you're not sure yourself, the protégé will get mixed messages from you;

- Look after your protégé's needs, but consider your own as well. Be certain about what you want from the relationship and what you're willing to give;

- Be prepared for the relationship to end. The successful mentor-protégé cycle requires that the protégé moves on and the relationship either ends or takes a different form.

Don'ts

- Don't give up right away if your protégé resists your help at first. It may take time to recognize the value of what you have to offer. Persistence - to a point - may help;

- Don't try to force your protégé to follow your footsteps. If the footsteps fit, the protégé will follow. Value the protégé's unique path as well;

- Don't have a pre-conceived plan for the final outcome of your relationship, leave room for growth.

Myths About the Mentor/Protégé Relationship
- The relationship benefits the protégé more than the mentor.

- Healthy mentor/protégé relationships won't run into difficulties.

Gems of Wisdom Imparted By Mentors & Protégés

Experience shows that many things can't be anticipated, no matter how diligently they may be researched in advance. There's a lot of learning that goes on in the relationship, some of it is planned and some happens serendipitously.

Current mentors and protégés impart the following *"gems of wisdom"* to help 8(a) firms learn from their experience.

■ Remember, reputation in a Mentor-Protégé relationship is a two-way street. When a protégé collaborates with a mentor the mentor's reputation affects the reputation of the protégé as well. Therefore, protégés should perform due diligence on the mentor and examine the mentor's experience in federal contracting. Ask questions about questionable matters, and if the mentor has previously mentored other protégé firms, interview those previously mentored firms to ascertain whether there were any problems in the relationship.

■ Make sure that the protégé and the mentor have the same definition of what constitutes mentoring. Remember, an approved Mentor-Protégé agreement is an extremely valuable resource; therefore, protégés have to be careful not to squander the opportunity and to ensure that they are in the right relationship.

■ Understand who in the mentor firm will be in charge of interacting with the protégé firm. Make sure that you develop good rapport with the responsible party or parties and understand the organizational structure of the mentor's firm to clarify which part or parts of the mentor's firm will be involved in the Mentor-Protégé relationship.

■ As former 8(a)BD graduate **Charito Kruvant** advised in the first *Gems of Wisdom* book, protégés should guard against being mesmerized by the mentor's firm; remember, the relationship has to be a two-way street. There must be room for the protégé to add value as well. If all the mentor firm is after is a way to gain access to contracts through the protégé firm, the relationship will not be productive.

■ As a key objective of the relationship for the protégé is growth, the protégé must be very clear at the outset about how the mentor will help the protégé grow. What will the mentor teach the protégé, how will knowledge be imparted, what knowledge will be imparted, and most importantly, as **Faye Fields**, former 8(a)BD graduate advised in the first *Gems of Wisdom* book: "Make sure the mentor firm really wants the protégé to grow. In this regard, develop "what if" scenarios and pose them to the mentor. For instance, "what if" the protégé pursues the same line of business as that of the mentor and the protégé wins a contract in a competition over the mentor, once the relationship ends—how would the mentor perceive such an occurrence? Or, supposed the protégé grows large enough to hire personnel from the mentor's firm, how would that be viewed by the mentor?

■ While certain mentoring functions can be anticipated in advance, ideally the relationship should evolve and change overtime and take into account the learning that happens in the beginning and therefore be able to accommodate new learning demands that facilitate growth. In other words, the relationship should be dynamic and growth oriented and its structuring should be flexible enough to accommodate the unexpected.

■ Having a clear understanding about what the mentor considers to be confidential and proprietary at the outset of the relationship can go a long way toward ensuring that any future relationship, once the agreement ends, will be positive and productive. Remember, the mentor firm is a possible strategic partner for the protégé firm long after the actual agreement expires. Thus, the protégé must take every measure and precaution required to remain in good standing with the mentor so that they can collaborate in the future.

■ Protégés should endeavor to put the mentoring advice into practice as soon as possible to demonstrate the utility and benefit of the relationship. At the same time, as learning and growing occurs within the protégé firm in the course of the relationship, the protégé should also endeavor to introduce new ideas and practices to the mentor as well. Believing in the principle that the whole is greater than the sum of the parts, together the mentor and protégé firm should be creating opportunities throughout the relationship that lead to an advancement of both firms along a number of different metrics.

■ In addition to the formal mentoring that goes on in the relationship there are opportunities inherent in the relationship for informal mentoring. Protégés should be mindful of this and seek out unanticipated learning opportunities associated with being involved with the mentor firm. Basically, the Mentor-Protégé is a gold mine: Protégés have to be good *gold miners*.

■ Constant monitoring, analysis, evaluation of and reflection on the relationship are keys to enabling protégé firms to be good *gold miners*.

■ Last but not least, the one *gem of wisdom* that outshines all others is that everything is about human relations. People have to like you and that holds true for mentors, government officials, and everyone with whom you come into contact. As **Rodney Hunt**, former successful 8(a)BD graduate, has noted, he can choose from the entire portfolio of 8(a) firms to select from as protégés. Mentors, however, will always select the one who has the sparkle in his eye, smile on his face, hunger in his belly, and the will and stamina to succeed. Therefore, be humble, be likable, and ensure that the *likeability quotient* **(LQ)** of your staff is as high as your own **because a high LQ will ultimately lead to a high ROI** (return on investment).

Once mentored, become a mentor. The 8(a)BD program and all of the business development resources it provides is a "hand up." As the old adage goes: "To he much is given, much is expected."

Answers to Frequently Asked Questions (FAQs) about the Mentor-Protégé Program can be found on SBA's website. A list of SBA-approved Mentor and Protégés is presented at the end of this chapter, together with a sample Mentor-Protégé Agreement.

List of SBA-Approved Mentors & Protégés

DISTRICT OFFICE	DATE APPROVED	MENTOR	PROTÉGÉ
New Mexico	05/24/02	3D International, Inc.	NEB, Inc.
Fresno	03/22/02	A.J. Diani Construction,Inc.	Rockwood General Contractors
Mississippi	06/04/04	AAI/ACL Technologies, Inc.	Applied Geo Technologies, Inc
Washington	06/28/00	ABLE Services Contractors, Inc.	Anda Services, Inc.
Santa Ana	11/01/04	ACE Engineering, Inc.	KNS Design Construction, Inc.
New Mexico	02/13/06	AJAC Enterprises	DLM Contracting Enterprises, Inc.
West Virginia	07/14/06	AK Supply, Inc.	REM Engineering Services
Alaska	10/05/00	AKAL Security	BNC Internationl Inc.
Alaska	07/14/06	Alaska Mechanical, Inc.	Nenana Lumber Company, Inc.
Cleveland	02/11/05	Albert Highley	KBJ. Inc
Hawaii	05/04/04	Albert Kobayashi, Inc	Biven's Electric d/b/a West Coast Construction
Alaska	07/25/00	Aliron International, Inc.	Tyonek Medical LLC
Washington	04/12/06	All Cities Enterprises	1st Cousins
Santa Ana	10/23/01	All Star Services, Inc.	MW Services, Inc.
North Florida	01/04/06	Alpha Data Corp.	Hixardt Technologies, Inc.
Dallas	02/24/06	Altech Services, Incorporated	NSYNC Services, Incorporated
New Mexico	12/11/06	AMEC Earth & Environmental, Inc.	Environmental Dimensions, Inc.
Illinois	06/17/03	American Demolition Corporation	Eason Environment Services
Sacramento	02/07/06	American Incorporated	Reva Murphy Associates
Washington	02/02/04	American Systems Corporation	DMS International, Inc/Data Management Services, Inc.
Illinois	12/09/05	Anthony Roofing Tecta America Co.	NWR Construction, Inc.
Washington	02/02/05	Apogen	Cambridge Communication Systems, Inc
Louisana	03/22/02	Applied Quality Communications, Inc.	Ultimate Solutions, Inc. (USI)
Washington	12/06/05	Apptis, Inc	ST Net, Inc
Boston	07/17/06	Arcadis, G&M, Inc.	The Bioengineering Group
Utah	09/27/02	ASET International Services Corp	Craig Enterprises, Inc. dba CommGap
Harlingen/Rio Grande	09/22/05	Asiel Enterprises, Inc.	Navales Enterprises, Inc.
Washington	03/03/05	Aspen Group, Inc.	Aspen of DC Inc.
Colorado	01/29/07	ATA Services, Inc.	Colorado Network Staffing Inc
Arizona	05/14/03	Atherton Construction, Inc.	Integrated Facility Construction and Management, Inc.
Illinois	03/22/02	Atkins Benham	Far East Construction
Arizona	06/10/05	Au Authum Ki Inc.	Nagaki Design Associates, Inc.
New Mexico	07/07/06	Austin Commerical, Inc.	Construction Technology Specialist, Inc.
Washington	03/03/04	Automated Resource Management Assoc.	Destiny Management Services LLC
Dallas	04/29/04	Aztec Facility Services, Inc.	Gylan Building Services Inc
Louisana	12/29/05	B+B Dredging Company	Sunset Marine, LLC
Washington	08/30/04	Base Technologies, Inc.	Trusted Mission Solutions Inc.
Houston	03/19/07	Basic Industries, Incorporated	All American Brothers Company, LLC
Richmond	08/18/05	Bay Electric Co., Inc.	M.C. Dean, Inc.
Minnesota	2/27/01	Belair Builders	Moltron Enterprises, Inc.
Portland	01/21/99	Benge Construction	Veraz Construction
Illinois	08/10/06	Berglund Construction	Acer Construction, Inc.
Washington	09/08/05	Betah Associates	Writeprocess Inc.
Alabama	04/05/06	Bhate Environmental Associates, Inc.	NationView, LLC

DISTRICT OFFICE	DATE APPROVED	MENTOR	PROTÉGÉ
Hawaii	01/31/02	Black Construction Corporation	Balanger & Associates, Inc.
Los Angeles	08/18/05	Blackstone Consulting, Inc.	Avery Group Inc
Alaska	08/18/05	Blackwater USA	Chenega Security and Protection Services
Tennessee	06/14/05	BMAR & Associates, Inc.	Electronic Metrology Laboratory, LLC
Georgia	11/08/02	Bradford & Byrd Associates, Inc.	Bi-Co Janitorial Co., Inc.
Los Angeles	09/28/05	Brown & Caldwell	American Integrated Services, Inc.
Alaska	05/22/01	Brown and Root Services	Olgoonik Management Services, LLC
Arizona	02/20/02	Brycom Corporation	RBG Construction
Seattle	07/12/06	Burton Construction	Eagle River
Arkansas	10/24/06	Byrd Brothers, Inc.	J. Gray Construction, Inc.
North Dakota	11/10/04	C & C Plumbing & Heating LLC	Roughrider Fire Suppression, Inc. d/b/a RFS, Inc.
Syracuse	03/22/06	C & S Engineers, Inc.	DevMar Associates
Georgia	01/28/00	C.J. Enterprise, Inc.	Cobb, Oliver F & Associates LLC
Louisiana	10/25/05	Cajun Contractors	Reeves Electrical Services, LLC
Alabama	05/16/05	CAMBER Corporation	Alpha Beta Technologies, Inc.
Georgia	10/04/05	Campbell Roofing	MGC Roofing & Construction, Inc.
Georgia	04/19/05	Cape Environmental Management, Inc.	EcoBlue, Inc.
Arizona	04/19/05	Cargill Meat	N'Genuity Enterprises Co
Oklahoma	09/29/04	Carothers Constructions	Tri-Con Roofing, Inc
Richmond	06/03/05	CAS, Inc	LPM, Incorporated
Colorado	02/25/04	CDM Federal Programs Corp.	PMTech, Inc.
Columbus	02/09/06	CDO Technologies, Inc.	Solutions Through Innovations Technologies, Inc.
Alaska	07/12/01	Centennial Contractor's Enterprise Inc.	Sentinel Industries
Kansas City	01/27/06	Ceres Environmental Services	James Kelly Construction Co.
Hawaii	02/26/01	Certified Construction, Inc.	Moriyama Construction Inc
Washington	03/09/06	CGI Federal, Inc.	ACE Info Solutions, Inc.
Alaska	07/25/02	CH2M HILL, INC.	AGVIQ, INC.
Sacramento	12/15/06	Chambers Group, Inc.	Burleson Consulting, Inc.
New Jersey	05/24/06	Cherokee Nations	PHACIL, INC.
Sacramento	11/03/06	CKY, Inc.	Huang & Associates, Inc
Washington	08/10/06	CM Construction, Inc.	General Services & Marketing, Inc.
Portland	06/19/06	CMI Management, Inc.	Ensoftek, Inc.
Dallas	08/03/05	Coachman Industries, Inc.	The Warrior Group Inc.
Maryland	12/07/05	Coakley & Williams Construction	Rich Moe Enterprises, LLC
San Antonio	05/06/06	Coastal Clinical & Management Services,	MEDTRUST LLC
New Mexico	07/14/06	Comforce Technical Services, Inc.	Technical Design, Inc.
Hawaii	05/23/00	Commercial Plumbing, Inc.	Yahiku Associates, Inc.
Washington	04/15/05	Consolidated Engineering Services, Inc.	Capitol Technology Services, Inc.
New York	09/11/06	Conti Environmental & Infrastructure, Inc.	Hirani Engineering & Landscaping, Inc.
Illinois	11/29/05	Contracting Consulting & Eng LLC	Vistas Construction of Illinois
Alaska	05/18/06	Cooper Zietz Engineers, Inc.	Bratslavsky Consulting Engineers, Inc
Alaska	08/18/06	Cornerstone Construction Co., Inc.	Kohtaene Enterprises Company, LLC
South Florida	02/14/05	Corporate Presentation Services, Inc.	Government Systems, Incorporated
New Mexico	01/07/04	Cortez III Service	Networx,Inc.
Washington	03/23/04	CRA Associates, Inc.	T Systems Group, LLC

DISTRICT OFFICE	DATE APPROVED	MENTOR	PROTÉGÉ
Louisana	05/22/01	Critique Resources Consulting Corp.	Deltha Corporation
Dallas	12/09/05	Crown Support Services, Inc.	Berry Logistics & Transportation, Inc.
Alabama	07/17/06	CSC Applied Technologies, Inc.	East West Enterprise, Inc.
Maryland	06/01/04	Cube Corp	Re-Engineered Business Solutions, Inc.
Washington	08/18/05	Cubic Applications, Inc.	Quantum Dynamics, Inc.
Santa Ana	04/29/02	Cumming LLC	Kanda Project Services, Inc.
Los Angeles	12/02/02	Curtom Building & Development	Alameda Construction Services, Inc.
Arizona	04/18/01	CYTEC Corporation	nFocus.com (SWMG)
Colorado	06/15/06	Daniel-Barry Construction, Inc.	Educational and Business Services, LLC
Washington	03/14/06	Data Solution & Technology Inc.	Amoorer Inc.
Dallas	08/22/03	Datatrac Information Services, Inc.	GWA Innovative Technology, Inc.
New Mexico	12/30/03	DDL Omni Engineering	Zia Engineering & E
San Diego	02/22/01	Del-Jen, Inc.	Project Resources Inc.
Washington	09/26/05	Delon Hampton & Associates, Chaterred (DHA)	OLBN Architectural Services, Inc.
Washington	06/06/06	Desbuild, Inc.	Beltsville Industries Group, Inc.
Washington	08/10/05	DevTech Systems, Inc.	Duca Consulting International
Washington	02/05/07	Digital Solutions, Inc.	Advanced Information Systems, Inc.
Columbus	02/17/04	Dimensions International, Inc.	Diversified Systems Inc
Alaska	06/23/04	Diversified Technology & Services of VA	Akima Intra-data, LLC
Los Angeles	09/08/04	DJM Construction Co., Inc.	MG Mako, Inc.
Detroit	03/08/01	DLZ Corporation	Altech Environmental Services, Inc.
South Dakota	01/28/00	DSMI General Contructors	C S DuBois Construction, Inc.
Houston	02/22/06	Duratek Federal Service , Inc.	TerranaerPMC, Inc.
Washington	11/06/06	Dynamic Corporation	Service All, Inc.
Fresno	08/14/03	Eagan, McAllister Associates	New Direction Technologies, Inc.
San Diego	06/28/01	Earl Industries, LLC	Epsilon Systems Solutions, Inc.
Tennessee	10/27/03	East Tennessee Mechanical Contractors	HME, Inc.
Richmond	04/18/01	Eastern Computers, Inc	C&C Technologies, Inc.
Alabama	01/12/06	EDAW Inc.	Kaya Associates
Santa Ana	06/16/01	Edge Development	Meza Builders
Alaska	02/02/04	EG&G Technical Services, Inc.	Goldbelt Eagle, LLC
Washington	06/30/05	EMS Consultants, Inc.	Falcon, Inc.
Colorado	03/04/05	Energetics	New West Technologies LLC
Washington	07/24/06	Engineering Application Consultants, Inc.	A-Thru-Z Inc.
Georgia	08/18/05	Engineering Design Technologies	Quality Design Carpentry
Colorado	07/15/04	Engineering-Environmental Mgmt., Inc.	Innovar Environmental Inc
Tennessee	11/15/05	Ensafe, Inc	Spectra Tech, Inc
Louisiana	01/22/07	Environmental Quality Management, Inc.	Quarternary Resource Investigations, Inc.
Richmond	02/23/06	Environmental Restoration Co.	Beaumon Industries, Inc.
Hawaii	03/29/06	Envisioneering, Inc.	Oceantronics, Inc.
Arizona	06/25/01	EPC Corporation	Candelaria General Engineering
Los Angeles	10/11/05	Equals Three Communications	Voices, Inc.
Dallas	05/01/07	Faith + Gould	Apex Cost Consultants, Inc.
Washington	07/01/05	FC Business Systems	Indigo Technology, Inc.
Buffalo	05/20/05	Ferguson Electric Holdings Corp.	American Rated Cable and Comm.
Oklahoma	04/08/05	Flintco, Inc.	CNI Construction, LLC

DISTRICT OFFICE	DATE APPROVED	MENTOR	PROTÉGÉ
Colorado	09/28/99	Foothill Engineering Consultants, Inc.	ATA Services, Inc.
Santa Ana	06/01/04	FPL and Associates, Inc.	WRC Consulting Services, Inc.
Dallas	12/19/05	Freese and Nichols, Inc.	Mulatech Engineering, Inc
Fresno	05/28/00	Garcia Roofing, Inc.	Vortex
San Antonio	07/24/06	Garco Contracting	Hinojsa Contracting
Alaska	05/20/04	Geat Northwest, Incorpoated	Denali Steel Erection, Inc.
Louisiana	03/15/06	GEC, Inc.	ECM Consultants
Los Angeles	03/20/06	Geomatrix Consultants, Inc.	Rubicon Engineering Corporation
Washington	06/18/04	Global Science & Technology	DB Consulting Group, Inc.
Colorado	02/22/01	Gonzales Consulting Services, Inc.	Spencer Williams & Associates
New York	04/22/03	Gottlieb Skanska, Inc.	Ortega General Contracting, Ltd.
Washington	11/03/05	GovConnection, Inc	Yancy & Associates Inc.
Tennessee	02/23/06	Government Telecommunications, Inc.	SECO Systems, Inc.
Washington	02/14/05	Grunley Construction Company, Inc.	Goel Services, Inc.
Alaska	07/16/02	GTSI Corporation	Eyak Technology, LLC.
Dallas	08/03/05	Halff Associates/ Arredondo	Arredondo, Zezeda and Brunz Inc
Georgia	01/03/06	Harbor Construction Co., Inc.	I.L. Fleming Construction, Inc.
Tennessee	12/19/01	Hardaway Construction Corporation	TG Inc.
Hawaii	11/15/02	Healy Tibbitts Builders, Inc.	American Piping & Boiler Company
New Jersey	07/02/07	Henkels & McCoy	West Bay Construction
Dallas	03/31/04	Hill & Wilkinson, LTD	Leetex Construction LLC
Louisiana	05/12/07	HNTB Corporation	Julien Engineering and Consulting, Inc.
Georgia	12/22/07	Holman Construction & General Contractors, Inc.	Jay's Home Construction, Inc.
Washington	07/24/06	HSU Development Company	Edifice Group, Inc.
Maryland	05/31/06	IFF Data Solutions, Inc.	A- Team Solutions, Inc.
Illinois	01/25/06	IHC Construction companies	Keyboard Enterprises, Inc.
New Jersey	02/26/01	Imperial Construction Group Inc.	Troop Construction & Electric, Inc.
Richmond	04/08/05	Indus Corporation	Arete Enterprises, Incorporated
North Florida	08/28/03	Intec Building Services, Inc.	Never Quit Enterprises, Inc.
New York	03/11/05	Integrated Construction Enterprises, Inc.	Goshow Architects
Seattle	12/11/06	Integrus Architecture, P.S.	Freeman Fong Architecture,P.S.
Alabama	05/23/00	Intergraph Federal Systems	Dale Technical Services
Hawaii	05/11/06	ITT Industries, Systems Division	Akimeka Technologies, LLC
Tennessee	11/21/05	J & S Construction Co. Inc.	Young, Jerry Construction, Inc.
Georgia	05/22/03	J&B Construction & Services, Inc.	Edlin Company, Inc.
San Antonio	07/31/03	J&J Maintenance, Inc.	Quality Services Int'l, LLC
Richmond	11/29/05	J.K. Hill & Associates, Inc.	ProLog, Inc.
Alaska	06/21/05	Jacobs Engineering Group	Chemtrack, LLC
Georgia	08/21/06	Jamison Professional Services, Inc.	Kera Enterprises
North Florida	01/25/04	Jardon and Howard Technologies, Inc.	A.I.W. Inc.
San Antonio	08/05/04	Jay Reese Contractors	ASD Consultants, Inc.
Philadelphia	11/04/03	Jeffrey Brown Associates, Inc.	Pride Enterprises, Inc.
Des Moines	07/26/01	JIL Information System Inc.	T.L. Grantham & Associates, Inc. (Intekras, Inc.)
Washington	06/19/06	Joe Ragan's Coffee, Ltd	Three Kids Enterprise, Inc.
Maryland	12/03/02	John Kirlin	Donley Construction
Mississippi	01/13/01	Johnson Controls, Inc	Dixon Interior Finishing

DISTRICT OFFICE	DATE APPROVED	MENTOR	PROTÉGÉ
Washington	04/13/04	Jones Technology, Inc.	Estime Enterprises, Inc.
Washington	06/26/03	Jorge Scientific Corporation	Cyberpath Inc.
Washington	03/08/01	Jupiter Corporation	Advanced Systems Technology & Management, Inc.
Santa Ana	11/19/04	KAL Architects, Inc.	Basilio Associates, Inc.
Montana	12/20/01	Keco Industries, Inc.	Pikuni Industries, Inc.
Alaska	08/10/01	Kellogg Brown & Root Services	KUK Construction, LLC
South Florida	07/16/99	Kohly Construction, Inc.	Michello, Inc.
Maryland	06/01/04	Konover Construction Corporation	BMW Construction Specialist, Inc.
Wisconsin	09/23/02	Kroeschell, Inc.	Belonger Corporation
Colorado	09/11/06	L&M Technologies, Inc.	Corporate Allocation Services, Inc.
Georgia	04/12/06	L. Robert Kimball & Associates, Inc.	Aiken Global Group, LLC
Washington	07/14/04	Laurel Consulting Group, Inc.	Wildon Solutions, LLC
Alaska	08/16/04	LB & B Associates, Inc.	Bering Straits AKI, LLC
Oklahoma	12/01/04	Leader Communications	A Plus Communications, Inc.
Alaska	05/10/05	Life Cycle Engineering, Inc.	Barling Bay,LLC
Richmond	01/05/04	Life Cycle Engineering, Inc.	ICI, LLC
Alabama	03/29/06	LJC Defense Contracting, Inc.	McClain Contracting Co., Inc.
Georgia	06/13/05	LLI Technologies, Inc.	Airtab, Inc.
Pittsburgh	09/06/06	Lockheed Martin Corporation	DynaCom Industries, Inc.
Alaska	10/20/04	Lockheed Martin Services, Inc.	KCorp Technology Services, Inc
Richmond	02/22/06	Logistics Management Resources, Inc.	Vision Point Systems, Inc.
San Antonio	07/12/06	Logmet, LLC	T-Squared Logistics Services
Illinois	12/15/99	Lori Construction,Inc.	Mozo, Inc.
Richmond	02/09/04	LTM, Inc.	DP Technology Services, Inc.
Colorado	07/14/06	Lucent Technologies, Inc.	Synchronized Networking Solutions, Inc.
Washington	06/19/06	Macro International, Inc.	The Baldwin Group, Inc.
Oklahoma	10/31/06	MACTEC Engineering	Muscogee Creek Nation
Washington	03/27/03	Madrid's Contracting, Inc.	Vigil Contracting Inc.
Houston	03/09/06	Malcolm Pirme, Inc.	PIKA International, Inc.
Los Angeles	09/24/02	Management Healthcare Prod	D.R. Group
Tennessee	03/11/04	Management Technology Associates, Inc.	Carter Safety Consultant, Inc.
Washington	10/24/03	ManTech Systems Engineering Corporatic	Enterprise Engineering, Inc.
Washington	09/21/05	Manufacturing Engineering Systems, Inc.	I Plus, Inc.
Alabama	12/05/01	Manufacturing Technology, Inc.	Muskogee Metal Works Inc.
San Antonio	12/17/04	Marco Enterprises	Marco Enterprises/ Maspero, Inc.
Nevada	02/14/03	Marnell Corrao Associates, Inc.	Avanced Demolition Tech. Inc.
Alaska	04/09/04	Marpac Construction, LLC	KIC Development, LLC
Hawaii	03/07/07	MARRS Services, Inc.	Donaldson Enterprises Inc
Santa Ana	06/30/06	Marrs Services, Inc.	ECO & Associates, Inc.
San Francisco	02/23/05	Martin Harris Construction	Marshall Dubas Construction
Colorado	06/15/06	Martinez International Corporation	Mesan, Inc.
Los Angeles	10/05/05	Massey Mechanical	MG Construction Management
Georgia	09/12/05	MAU, Inc.	Dover Staffing, Inc.
El Paso	06/06/03	MCC Construction Corporation	JACO General Contractors, Inc.
Hawaii	12/07/05	McDonald & Wetle Inc	Affordable Roofing & Repair LTD.
Colorado	04/08/05	MCDS,Inc	The Centurion Group, Inc.
Kansas City	10/12/05	Mckinzie Construction	ABS Support Services, Inc

DISTRICT OFFICE	DATE APPROVED	MENTOR	PROTÉGÉ
Georgia	03/08/04	McKnight Construction Company, Inc.	Utley Construction, Inc.
Cleveland	01/11/05	Mega-Tech, Inc.	Trega-Tech, Inc.
Hawaii	05/22/03	MELE Associates, Inc.	Yamasato Fujuwara Higa & Associates, Inc
Tennessee	08/31/06	Merrick & Company	Innovative Design Inc.
San Antonio	06/20/06	Metrica, Inc.	Netgineer Data Systems, Inc.
Kansas City	12/15/04	Michaelson, Conner & Go	Greenleaf Construction Co., Inc.
Illinois	01/15/03	Mid-American Elevator Company, Inc.	Phoenix Elevator Co., Inc.
El Paso	07/25/00	Mike Garcia Merchant Security, Inc	RBH Sec. & Investigations, Inc
Columbus	08/18/05	Miles-McClellan Construction Company, Inc.	Reid Plumbing, LLC
North Florida	07/03/03	Military Construction Corporation	Quality Electrical Services, Inc.
Kansas City	12/01/00	Mill Valley	HMC Enterprise Corporation
Nebraska	11/15/00	Miller Electric Company	Channell Construction Company, Inc.
El Paso	08/05/05	Miratek Corp.	Vargas, PC
Alaska	04/12/06	MKB Constructors	L & N Ventures
Arizona	06/09/06	Motorola, Inc.	Solomon Technical Solutions, Inc.
North Florida	08/19/99	MTI Construction Company Inc.	General Precision Manufacturing Inc.
Montana	04/10/03	MTM Contractors, Inc.	Barnes Construction Services
Dallas	03/09/06	N E Construction, LTD	Murillo Modular Group, Ltd
Arkansas	05/19/05	Nabholz Construction	Jack Morgan Construction
Kentucky	09/11/06	NAC Heavy Highway, Inc.	K. Hayes Limited
Hawaii	08/31/06	Nan, Inc.	SU-MO Builders, Inc.
Tennessee	09/27/05	Navarro Research & eng. Inc.	Gem Tech
Washington	04/13/04	Network Engineering, Inc	Gentry Systems Incorporated
Philadelphia	05/11/05	Norfolk Dredging Co.	Coleman Construction Company Inc
South Dakota	03/16/01	Northern Improvement Co.	Aqua-Envirotech Mfg. Inc.
North Florida	08/14/01	Northwest Florida Facilites Management, I	The Orasa Group Inc.
Santa Ana	06/30/05	Oakview Construction	Gonzales, Suarez & Associates, Inc.
Utah	10/15/02	Okland Construction Co., Inc.	Saiz Construction Co., Inc.
Tennessee	11/06/06	Omniplex World Services Corporation	Netgain Corporation
Washington	03/31/06	OnPoint Consulting, Inc.	Tantus Technologies, Inc.
Washington	04/06/06	Optimos, Inc.	Shiva Information Tech. Services, Inc.
South Dakota	01/23/03	Ostrom Painting & Sandblasting, Inc.	Tsa La Gi, Inc.
Richmond	06/06/06	Owens & Minor Medical, Inc.	Mirror Enterprise, Inc.
Washington	04/23/06	Pal Tech	IT Shows Inc.
Washington	11/10/04	Paradigm Solution Corp.	PowerTek Corporation
Georgia	04/13/07	Paragon Systems, Inc.	On Duty Patrol Service, Inc. (ODPS)
New York	06/30/06	PCCI, Inc.	Coastal Environmental Group, Inc.
Seattle	03/27/03	PCL Construction Services	JKT Development, Inc.
Louisana	05/05/06	Penn Environmental & Remediation, Inc.	Smart, Incorporated
Philadelphia	03/16/06	Pennoni Associates, Inc.	Progressive Engineering Group, LLC
Seattle	01/28/05	Performance Abatement Services, Inc.	Net Compliance Environmental
North Florida	01/18/05	Perry Roofing, Inc.	Kemper Marketing, Inc.
Houston	08/16/06	Phoenix Management	Hallmark Capital Group, LLC
Illinois	04/02/04	Pickus Construction	Chicago Architectural Metals,Inc.
Washington	04/27/06	Planners Collaborative, Inc.	6K Systems, Inc.
Illinois	02/20/02	Plexus Scientific Corp.	MG Simmons &Associates

DISTRICT OFFICE	DATE APPROVED	MENTOR	PROTÉGÉ
Houston	09/21/05	PolySpec, LP	Linda Gonzalez P.C.
Pittsburgh	07/25/06	Power Contracting Company	Vantage Corporation
Richmond	06/15/06	Preferred System Solutions, Inc.	Eastern System Research, Inc.
San Antonio	10/05/05	Premier Inc.	Preferred Consulting, Inc.
New Mexico	01/23/03	Pride Industries	Quality Maintenance
Georgia	06/29/06	Protech Contractors, Inc.	Vastec Group, Inc.
Washington	01/24/07	PRO-telligent,LLC	Prime Source Technologies,LLC
Alaska	04/13/06	PULAU Electronics Corp.	Tatitlek Support Services
Dallas	01/25/06	Qnet Information Services	Telecommunication Consultants Services Inc
Georgia	06/06/06	R. L. Campbell Roofing Co.,	Johnson Roofing & Construction
Puerto Rico	08/24/06	Ready and Responsible Security, Inc.	Advance Investigation Group, Inc.
Richmond	12/05/03	Regent Systems, Inc.	Favor Network Services, LLC
Washington	01/24/06	REI Systems, Inc.	Ebits Corporation
Richmond	09/26/05	Reid Associates, Inc.	Robra Construction, Inc.
Kentucky	05/31/05	Reliable Contracting Group, LLC	TEM Electric, Inc.
Washington	07/07/06	RER Solutions, Inc.	Benefits Consulting Associates, Inc.
New Mexico	02/09/06	Research Analysis & Maintenance, Inc.	Analytican F.E.A., Inc.
Los Angeles	09/24/02	Reyes Construction, Inc.	Miramar Construction
San Antonio	03/22/02	Riojas Enterprises, Inc.	Career Quest
New Mexico	11/07/02	RMCI	Sam Con, Inc.
Santa Ana	06/01/04	Rogan Building Services, Inc.	Dynamic Building Services
San Diego	01/29/07	Rogers Quinn Construction, Inc.	Richard Brady & Associates, Inc.
Maryland	12/08/03	Roy Kirby and Sons, Inc.	Eclipse Construction and Painting, Inc
Washington	11/10/04	RS Information Systems	1 Source Consulting, Inc.
New York	08/30/06	S & E Services, Inc.	Complete Technical Service, Inc.
Richmond	02/22/06	S.B. Ballard Construction Company	Ocean Construction Services, Inc.
Colorado	01/26/05	S.M. Stoller Corporation	JG Management Systems, Inc.
Tennessee	02/28/01	Safety and Ecology Corporation	Spectrum Inc.
Washington	06/06/06	Sanders Brothers Inc.	Advanced Engineering Design, Inc.
Kentucky	06/01/00	Sang Corporation	Leong Enterprises
Alabama	09/18/06	Science & Engineering, Inc.	Superior Solutions
North Florida	02/09/04	Science and Management Resources, Inc.	Aviation Systems of NW Florida, Inc.
Dallas	01/21/04	Science Application International Corporation	E Quality Corporation
Washington	05/20/05	Science Systems & Applications, Inc.	Mayur Technologies, Inc.
San Francisco	03/16/01	Security U S A Inc.	Side Bar Associates
San Antonio	12/17/05	Selrico Services	DSC Cleaning, Inc.
Washington	12/09/05	SGT, Inc	Sigma Space Coporation
New Mexico	07/02/03	Shaw Environmental	Portage Environmental
Colorado	12/13/06	SI International, Inc.	Summit Technical Solutions, LLC
North Carolina	09/11/06	SIGCOM, Inc.	STA Technologies, Inc.
Alaska	07/08/02	SKE Support Services, Inc.	Ukpik LLC
Alaska	01/12/01	SKW/Eskimos, Inc.	Caddo Construction LLC
Alaska	06/28/01	Sodexho Management, Inc.	Nana Servoces, LLC
Illinois	04/19/05	Sollitt, George Construction Company	Charpie Construction, Inc.
Alabama	06/29/04	Solutions to Environmental Problems, Inc.	Great Southern Engineering

DISTRICT OFFICE	DATE APPROVED	MENTOR	PROTÉGÉ
Georgia	04/11/03	South Georgia Cleaning Service, Inc.	U.S. Cleaning Services Etc., Inc.
Georgia	04/14/04	Southeastern Facility Management, Inc.	Facility Management International,Inc.
Kansas City	01/10/06	Spencer Reed Group, Inc.	Elite Computer Consultants Corp.
Los Angeles	08/18/05	St. Mortiz Security Services, Inc.	Picore & Associates Inc.
Seattle	03/02/07	Straightline Construction, Inc.	Quality Woodworking & Construction, LLC
Los Angeles	02/02/06	Sullivan International Group	Allied Industries Inc
Oklahoma	02/16/05	Summit Contractors	CND, LLC
New Mexico	12/19/03	Swinerton Builders, Inc.	Builtek Contractors, Inc.
Maryland	01/21/99	System Eng. & Associates, Inc.	New Concept Inc.
Nevada	05/04/04	T.N. & Associates, Inc.	Barajas & Associates, Inc.
Houston	04/13/07	Team Housing Solutions, Inc.	Kimrick Financial, LLC
Santa Ana	03/21/07	Technology & Management Services, Inc.	Performance Excellence Partners, Inc.
New Mexico	01/14/04	Tecumseh Professional Associates, Inc.	Keres Consulting, Inc.
Arizona	05/11/06	Telecom Remarketing Corporation of America	Netsis,LLC
Arizona	09/28/99	Teltara,Inc	Integrated Technology Works, Inc.
Illinois	10/28/05	Teng Construction, LLC	Spann Tech, Inc
New Mexico	03/23/05	Terradigm, Inc	Saavedra & Rice, PA
Richmond	11/06/06	Tesoro Corporation	Construction Development Services, Inc.
Maryland	01/15/04	Tessada & Associates, Inc.	Beacon & Associates, Inc.
San Diego	03/26/03	Tetra Tech EM, Inc.	Sullivan Consulting Inc.
Washington	04/20/07	The Arora Group, Inc.	Absolute Staffers, LLC
Oklahoma	12/11/06	The Benham Companies, LLC	Cherokee CRC, LLC
Richmond	07/12/05	The Bionetics Corp.	Goldbelt Falcon, LLC
Washington	07/03/06	The Centech Group, Inc.	Harman Systems, Inc.
New Jersey	09/21/05	The Louis Berger Group, Inc.	Pars Environmental, Inc.
Illinois	09/10/02	The Pickus Companies	T. Wallace Blacktopping
North Florida	06/06/00	The Tower Group	N.P. Construction of North FL, Inc.
Illinois	09/28/01	The Walsh Group	Broadway Consolidation
Tennessee	06/06/03	The Weitz Company	Sherrick Construction, Inc.
South Carolina	12/13/06	The Winter Construction Company	Universal Supplies & Service
Washington	08/09/06	Thomas Computer Solutions	Invizion, Inc.
Los Angeles	06/15/04	Thomas Land Clearing Company	Walter Thomas & Associates
San Antonio	10/26/05	Tino's Welding & Fabrication	Davilla Construction, Inc
Tennessee	08/31/05	TMS Contracting, LLC	R L Alvarez Construction Company
Oklahoma	08/23/03	Todd Construction	White Hawk Group, INC
Indiana	04/26/06	TolTest , Inc.	Custom Mechanical Systems, Corp
Colorado	08/18/06	Torix General Contractors, LLC	B&M Construction, Inc.
Houston	08/15/05	Trajen Systems, LP,Inc.	Torres Associates dba Sustainment Technologies
South Carolina	03/16/04	Trane Comfort Solutions	Randolph Technology, Inc.
Washington	11/18/04	Transporation management Services,Inc.	Private Executive Services, Inc.
Washington	02/14/05	Trax Intl. Corporation	Dozier Technologies
Seattle	05/06/05	Triton Marine Construction Corp.	Freitas Construction Corp.
Alaska	02/10/04	Turner Collie & Braden, Inc.	Inuit Services, Inc.
Illinois	10/23/01	UBM, Inc.	Sarang, Inc.

DISTRICT OFFICE	DATE APPROVED	MENTOR	PROTÉGÉ
Washington	10/24/03	Ultra Technologies, Inc.	Networking & Engineering Technologies Inc.
South Dakota	06/28/01	Uniband, Inc.	Arrow-Tech, Inc.
Montana	06/06/03	United Materials, Inc.	Three Way Construction, Inc.
Washington	12/15/06	University Research Company, LLC	Midego
Georgia	09/11/06	Urban Services Group, Inc.	JHS Cleaning, Inc.
North Carolina	01/17/03	URS Corporation	ESA Environmental Specialists, Inc.
Washington	08/07/06	US Protect Corporation	Trinity Protection Services, Inc.
South Florida	01/04/06	V W International, Inc.	Sentry Barricades, Inc.
Tennessee	07/07/06	Veit & Company	Tarraf Construction Inc.
Washington	06/06/06	W. M. Scholsser Construction, Inc.	Meltech Corporation
Illinois	08/19/02	W.E. O'Neil	Extra Clean (EDI)
Richmond	07/12/05	W.M. Jordan Co. Inc.	Homeland Contracting Corp.
North Carolina	07/10/02	W.T. Humphrey,Inc.	Kinston Contracting, Inc.
Washington	08/29/06	Walbridge Aldinger Company	Future Care LLC
Washington	07/05/07	Walton Construction	TMG Services, Inc.
Richmond	02/15/05	Webb Technologies	Wilder Mechanical, Inc.
Pittsburgh	06/05/05	Wellington Power Corporation	Advanced Integration Group, Inc.
Tennessee	08/18/05	Weskem	Environmental, Safety & Health, Inc.
New Mexico	01/03/06	Westech International, Inc.	GenQuest, Inc.
Arizona	07/12/05	Western Roofing Service	Atlas Construction Services
San Francisco	04/06/05	Westinghouse Govt. Services	Innovative Technical Solutions
Boise	07/31/03	Weston Solutions, Inc.	North Wind, Inc
Alaska	03/22/06	Wilder Construction Company	Ancor, Inc.
Utah	12/21/05	Yash Technologies, Inc.	Suh'dutsing Technologies LLC
Santa Ana	06/03/04	Yeager Shanska, Inc.	CGO Construction Company, Inc.
Richmond	05/17/05	Zel Technologies	E&E Enterprises Global, Inc.

Mentor/Protégé Agreement Template

Mentor/Protégé Agreement

between

ABC (Protégé)

and

XYZ (Mentor)

This Mentor/Protégé Agreement ("Agreement") is between **ABC** ("Protégé), a Louisiana State corporation with its principal place of business at 12345 Alpha Brooks Drive, Suite 211, New Orleans, Louisiana 70816, and **XYZ** ("Mentor"), a Virginia Corporation 16789 Beta Block Lane, Suite 550, Chantilly, Virginia 20151 (collectively referred to as the "Parties").

WHEREAS, **ABC** (Protégé) is a SBA-certified 8(a) Business Development BD) Program participant performing in North American Industry Classification System (NAICS) codes (*include NAICS number and title*) _____ specializing in providing _____. (*Provide a brief description of the Protégé's capability in performing in its primary NAICS code.*)

WHEREAS, **XYZ** (Mentor) is a corporation with a history of providing diversified services in (*Provide a brief description of the Mentor's technical capabilities and contracting history, especially with the Federal Government*).

WHEREAS, the Parties wish to formalize the proposed Mentor/Protégé relationship between **XYZ** (Mentor) and **ABC** (Protégé) under the U.S. Small Business Administration's ("SBA") Mentor/Protégé Program established pursuant to 13 C.F.R. §124.520; and

WHEREAS, the Parties agree that establishing a Mentor/Protégé relationship can enhance the capabilities of the Protégé and improve its ability to successfully compete for contracts consistent with the goals of SBA's Mentor/Protégé Program; and "material benefits" and "developmental gains"

WHEREAS, the Protégé certifies that it does not have another Mentor

WHEREAS, the Protégé can greatly benefit from the assistance that the Mentor proposes to offer, and the Mentor is qualified to provide the "material benefits," "developmental gains," and assistance within the context o the SBA Mentor/Protégé Program; and

WHEREAS, the Parties wish to carry out the goals of this Agreement and the Mentor proposes to provide such assistance as detailed below for at least one year per 13 C.F.R. § 124.520(e)(1).

THEREFORE, consistent with the Parties goals and the requirement of the SBA Mentor/ Protégé Program, the Parties agree to the following:

1. <u>Assessment of the Protégé's Needs.</u> As an 8(a) company seeking to develop a business base and infrastructure to successfully participate and graduate from the 8(a) BD Program as a viable company, the Protégé requires assistance in the following areas (*The Protégé should identify each area of assistance needed and show how this assistance will assist in meeting the business plan targets, goals and objectives, as stated in the SBA-approved business plan*):

    a. Management and technical assistance
    Meets objectives of business plan (SBA Form 1010C) paragraph _____

    b. Financial assistance
    Meets objectives of business plan (SBA Form 1010C) paragraph _____

    c. Business development assistance
    Meets objectives of business plan (SBA Form 1010C) paragraph _____

    d. Contracting assistance.
    Meets objectives of business plan (SBA Form 1010C) paragraph _____

    e. General and administrative assistance
    Meets objectives of business plan (SBA Form 1010C) paragraph _____

2. Mentor agrees to assist the Protégé to fully develop the assessed needs as described in paragraph 1 above pursuant to 13 C.F.R. § 124.520. (*Mentor must describe in detail how it will provide the assessed needs of the Protégé and when*).

    a. Management and technical assistance.
      i. *Assistance the Mentor will provide*
      ii. *TIMELINE*

    b. Financial assistance.
      i. *Assistance the Mentor will provide*
      ii. *TIMELINE*

    c. Business development assistance.
      i. *Assistance the Mentor will provide*
      ii. *TIMELINE*

    d. Contracting assistance.
      i. *Assistance the Mentor will provide*
      ii. *TIMELINE*

    e. General and administrative assistance.
      i. *Assistance the Mentor will provide*
      ii. *TIMELINE*

3. <u>Preparation of Mentor/Protégé Reports.</u> The Mentor shall use its reasonable and best efforts to assist the Protégé in preparation of the annual Mentor/ Protégé report required by the SBA pursuant to 13 C.F.R. §124.520(f), and shall provide all necessary documentation SBA requires.

4. <u>Terms of the Agreement.</u> Mentor agrees to provide such assistance to the Protégé for at least one year pursuant to 13 C.F.R. §124.520(e)(1). Continuation of the Agreement is contingent upon SBA's review of the Protégé's report on the Mentor/Protégé relationship as part of its annual review of the firm's business plan pursuant to 13 C.F.R. §124.403.

5. <u>Termination Clause.</u> This Agreement may be terminated as follows:

      i. <u>Voluntary Termination by the Mentor.</u> Pursuant to 13 C.F.R. §124.520(e)(3), the Mentor may voluntarily terminate this agreement if the Mentor no longer wishes to participate in the Program as a Mentor to a Protégé. The Mentor shall notify the Protégé and the SBA in writing at least 30 days prior to the termination date.

      ii. <u>Voluntary Termination by the Protégé.</u> Pursuant to 13 C.F.R. §124.520(e)(3), the Protégé may voluntarily terminate this Agreement if the Protégé no longer wishes to participate in the Program as a Protégé to a Mentor. The Protégé shall notify the Mentor and the SBA in writing at least 30 days prior to the termination date.

       iii.   **Termination by the SBA.** Pursuant to 13 C.F.R. §124.520(f)(3), SBA may decide not to approve continuation of the Agreement if it finds that the Mentor has not provided the assistance set forth in the Agreement or that the assistance has not resulted in any "material benefit" or "developmental gains" to the Protégé.

6.   **Effect of Termination.** Termination of this Agreement shall not impair the obligations of the Mentor to perform its contractual obligations pursuant to government rime contracts being performed with the Protégé. Likewise, termination of this Agreement shall not impair the obligations of the Protégé to perform its contractual obligations under any current contract or subcontracts between the Mentor and Protégé.

7.   **Modifications.** Pursuant to 13 C.F.R. § 124.520(e)(5), SBA must approve all changes to this Agreement in advance.

8.   **Notices and Points of Contact for the SBA Program Administration.** The following individuals shall serve as the points of contact for administration of the Agreement and as such are authorized to receive all notices under this Agreement.

XYZ (Mentor)	ABC (Protégé)
Name/Title	Name/Title
16789 Beta Block Lane,	12345 Alpha Brooks Drive
Suite 550	Suite 211
Chantilly, VA 20151	New Orleans, LA 70816
Telephone	Telephone
Fax	Fax
Email	Email

9.   **Status of the Parties.** This Agreement, in and of itself, does not constitute, create or give effect to or otherwise establish a joint venture agreement, partnership, or any other business or organization. Unless provided by the terms of another agreement consistent with the governing regulations, the Parties are and shall remain independent contractors.

10.   **Integrated Document.** This Agreement supersedes any and all previous understandings, commitments, or agreements, oral or written, pertaining to the SBA Mentor/Protégé Agreement.

11.   **Other Provisions not Previously Discussed (if applicable):**

       Subject to the approval of the U.S. Small Business Administration's Associate Administrator for Business Development, this Agreement is entered into and effective as of the date of such approval. The Agreement is officially signed and executed by officials duly authorized to bind the named corporations this _____ day of _____, 20XX.

       _____   _____
       Signatory, **ABC** (Protégé)   Signatory, **XYZ** (Mentor)
       Signatory Information   Signatory Information

       Date _____   Date _____

_____

Charito Kruvant (Creative Associates)
"It's all about excellence and EXCEL—in addition to mastering your craft, you must master the art of business management."

Rodney Hunt (RSIS)
"We always viewed ourselves as a Fortune 500 company from day one in the program and we approached everything we did, from preparing our business plan, to marketing agencies as if we were already a Fortune 500 firm."

Pat Parker (NAMS)
"If you want to succeed in the 8(a) BD program and *beyond*, find your passion and a good accountant."

Delores Fisk (Mega-Tech)
"Be a prism through which light can flow: Don't get in the way, listen, learn, and match yourself to what is needed."

Wayne Gatewood (Quality Support)
"Remember that when you provide services you are a servant; be humble and have integrity in all that you do."

Wendell Maddox (ION Corporation)
"When you are operating alone you have one set of resources, when you join forces with others you have twice as much power: Everyone should have strategic partners because you cannot compete in today's environment without them."

Faye Fields (IRT)
"Gain a reputation for whatever helps you win."

Carlo Lucero (Sparkle Maintenance)
"Doing nothing to win business is not a strategy."

Dr. Faye Coleman (Westover Consultants)
"When you prepare your business plan picture what success is, keep it in mind, and be true to your vision."

Charito Kruvant

Creative Associates

Rodney Hunt

Pat Parker

Gems of Wisdom

for Succeeding in the 8(a) BD Program— *and Beyond*

RSIS   NAMS

Delores Fisk   Wayne Gatewood

Mega-Tech   Quality Support

Wendell Maddox   Faye Fields

ION Corporation   IRT

Faye Coleman   Carlo Lucero

Westover Consultants Sparkle Maintenance

AASBEA PUBLISHERS
www.aasbea.com